Flora McEvedy read History at Oxford University before completing a law degree. She was called to the Bar in 1997, practising family-based law. She is married and has two stepdaughters, plus three children of her own.

The Step-parents' Parachute

Flora McEvedy

TIME WARNER
BOOKS

TIME WARNER BOOKS

First published in Great Britain in September 2005 by
Time Warner Books

A CIP catalogue record for this book
is available from the British Library.

ISBN 0 316 73029 7

Typeset in Palatino by M Rules
Printed and bound in Great Britain
by Clays Ltd, St Ives plc

Time Warner Books
An imprint of
Time Warner Book Group UK
Brettenham House
Lancaster Place
London WC2E 7EN

www.twbg.co.uk

To my stepdaughters,
the inspiration for this book

Contents

Acknowledgements

All the willing step-parents and stepchildren who agreed to be interviewed share the credit for this book. Their experiences gave depth and range to what is an extraordinarily varied subject. Talking to these men and women, youngsters and adults alike, added a tremendous amount to my own story.

My researchers, Esther Walker and Henry Lamb, were fantastically helpful and diligent. My editor, Joanne Dickinson, was unbelievably patient as I missed repeated deadlines. Her wonderful calmness was a tonic. And my agent Claire Patterson deserves praise for nursing a germ of an idea into something that had life.

The kindness of The Mind Gym team was also impressive. They gave authority to the self-assessment questionnaire in Chapter 2, being generous both with their time and expertise. I am indebted to them.

Finally, my husband deserves a mention for exercising great tolerance as this project grew tentacles into our home.

Flora McEvedy
London
May 2005

Foreword

by Dr Miriam Stoppard

The besetting problem of being a step-parent is that it calls on us to be more generous, more selfless than we have a natural tendency to be. That's what makes it so difficult a role to fill well. At one time or another it involves the suspension of all the rules and expectations of reciprocity, rules that we've come to believe in since we were children. It's as if the usual contracts of human behaviour had never evolved.

Step-parenthood is nearly always thrust upon us, as is the new grouping, the stepfamily. It's called a family but it comes with none of the familiar trappings. The cement that holds families together is missing. There's no commonality to fall back on, no shared history, no easy telegraphese, no old family jokes.

Underpinning our inferior status in this setting is the absence of a blood relationship with our stepchildren which would give us automatic rights. The uncomfortable truth is we have no rights, we are stateless.

A stepfamily is a discontinuity, and as such leads us to abandon self-belief and suspend rational behaviour.

Until now step-parenting came with no handbook. The only model we have had is motherhood or fatherhood, and to chase after that ideal is unrealistic and not very helpful. Being a step-parent brings a whole raft of issues one never has to face as a parent and it's figuring out how to deal with these egregious difficulties that can be so painful.

What every step-parent needs is a road map, complete with signposts marking where the minefields lie. Twice in my life I've wished for such a hitchhiker's guide, when I found myself taking on stepchildren in very different circumstances – the first with two baby boys, the second with two grown-up, sophisticated young women, occasions separated by more than twenty years but each requiring a skill set I'd yet to master.

Well, here it is – the must-have guide for anyone with the prospect of becoming a step-parent and the one I wish I'd had on my bedside table on both occasions. Open it on any page and you'll find a description of exactly what you're feeling and an insight that will resolve your quandary.

As step-parents most of us are our own worst enemies, aiming at standards that are well nigh impossible to achieve, setting ourselves up for failure and falling prey to self doubt, followed closely by plummeting self-esteem and a deep sense of having fallen short.

What is so reassuring about this book is the candour of its admissions. Flora McEvedy doesn't shrink from examining the darkest forces at play in a step-parent's mind. We've all been there but it's cathartic to acknowledge that our most uncharitable thoughts and emotions are common to all of us.

No matter how pusillanimous your reactions have been, no matter how shamingly hostile your feelings towards your stepchildren, they're all here, laid bare, uncompromisingly. It takes a brave person to admit to reverberating anger, guilt, envy, jealousy, self-pity and resentment but this author does so on behalf of us all. Admission is the prequel to healing and this book is packed with curative strategies and rational approaches.

We all need coping mechanisms and McEvedy presents us with sound principles that promise to convert us into the step-parent we long to be. She refers to them as the four cornerstones, which, by providing you with a new pair of spectacles to view your role, will free you from deadly negative emotions:

The antidote to *jealousy* is to remember YOU AND YOUR PARTNER ARE A TEAM (insurmountable if you work together).

Dealing with *resentment* is made easy if you KNOW YOUR ROLE and accept it (you will never be the equal of their parents).

You won't take *hostility* personally if you KEEP REJECTION AT ARM'S LENGTH (and you'll be free of a destructive line of thought).

Your self-image and confidence will stay intact if you remember YOUR STEPCHILDREN NEED YOUR LOVE (and you'll start to trust each other).

With a poignant examination of her own behaviour towards her stepchildren, McEvedy shows how these cornerstones interconnect to form a virtuous circle. Her courage and frankness are inspirational. And then there's the bonus of her exquisite prose style.

The Step-parents' Parachute

1

Introduction

In years gone by, when we imagined our futures, not many of us envisaged ourselves ending up as step-parents. And yet here we are, committed to a partner who has children from a previous relationship. Although we have all chosen our partner, none of us has chosen our stepchildren.

Despite this obvious fact, we do have some choice. We can elect to make a go of things with these youngsters who have their own reservations about us. Not that we need to be their best friend or their surrogate mother or their replacement father – but we do need to get along, to live in some kind of harmony and be allowed to enjoy life. All we need is something workable.

When I first became a stepmother to my partner's little daughters, then aged six and two, I thought that coming up with something workable would be easy enough. They lived near by with their mother and would come to stay with us every weekend, occasionally the odd weeknight too.

What I hadn't bargained for was their extreme hostility to Daddy's new girlfriend. They simply did not want me around. As far as they were concerned, having me in the house meant sharing their dad, and this was not something they were prepared to do. Their resistance was a dark counterweight to my optimism. These children were still feeling the aftershock of their parents' divorce.

For a couple of years, we were paralysed, cut loose in a drift of uncertainty. Blame spiralled out of control. My stepdaughters were determined to keep me out of their space with their daddy, even though by this stage we already had one child together. Defeated, I was left wondering where to turn.

Casting about for help, I found many texts that described step-family turmoil but I did not find what I was looking for: a straightforward guide to turning around a bad dynamic. The absence of anything constructive forced me to concentrate. There had to be a way to resolve what is after all an everyday problem. Why then was I so confused?

Life with my stepdaughters was like walking the tightrope: a precarious business with me in constant danger of losing it as I tried to balance their needs against my own, seemingly con-flicting, needs. Right from the start we were coming at this situation from radically different directions. I wanted to be wel-comed in, whereas they wanted to barricade me out. My priorities could not take precedence but on the other hand I did not want to be dominated. Wobbling along that thin line was quite a feat.

As a lawyer who practised in family law, I was familiar with all the aggro that could erupt in a domestic setting – the custody bat-tles and contact disputes had all been part of a day's work – but now I was exposed to this kind of strife in my own home, as we struggled to reconcile opposing forces. I don't know whether it was my legal training or a peculiar aspect of my character that urged me on to try to regularise the chaos and pull back from the brink. I just didn't want to be a loathed stepmother.

These days both my stepdaughters are a real pleasure to me. However, if someone had told me at the beginning of my step-mothering life that these two little girls would one day love me, I would have laughed them out of town. Having gone through some rather alarming teething problems, we have well and truly come out the other side. At our wedding a couple of years back, these two girls trotted down the aisle behind us, along with my biological kids tripping over my dress.

The four cornerstones set out in this book became clear to me over time. This is not the work of an expert: it is simply the experience of someone who has lived through some awful step-parenting lows and wanted to reach the highs. It is plain common sense, not rocket science. The approach is broad-brush, to tackle the big issues that underpin a stepfamily rather than attempt to address the specifics of every possible situation. Other texts out there focus more on the nitty-gritty mechanics, notably Erica Lutz's *Complete Idiot's Guide to Stepparenting* (Alpha Books, 1998).

Being a step-parent is a steep learning curve. It's no different from natural parenthood in this regard: you have suddenly acquired a huge responsibility and it's not one that you can walk away from. Just as a biological parent must embrace a whole new world of practical and emotional obligations, a step-parent must face up to the complex dynamics of stepfamily life. If we do not want to sink, we must learn to swim.

Unfortunately, when it comes to raising the next generation our contribution goes largely unnoticed. And yet we have a vital part to play, frequently shouldering a large amount of the co-parenting work, often more than a non-custodial bioparent. This is especially true of step-parents who live full-time with their stepchildren. They deserve much more recognition than they receive.

There has to be a reason for this lack of recognition. It is a harsh truth that society only values the parenting work that is provided by an actual bioparent. The additional support supplied by a step-parent is rarely something that society is happy to acknowledge. Step-parents remain marginal figures, skulking on the sidelines, almost embarrassed by their role. Yet by hovering in the shadows we are acquiescing in the negative attitudes about step-parents ingrained into our culture. It's time to come out of obscurity and walk tall. We should be proud of what we have to offer.

A step-parent works hard for the benefit of partner and stepchildren, but entrenched prejudice makes step-parenting something of a thankless task. This wider bias can often amplify what we are experiencing in the home, as we bend over backwards for stepchildren who want little to do with us. We put in the manpower but without receiving any satisfaction, let alone thanks. Quickly we begin to wonder what the rewards of step-parenting could possibly be. This thorny question is at the heart of most of our difficulties. There is certainly no general social endorsement of step-parenthood as there is for natural parenthood. Raising stepchildren has no status.

Where then does the satisfaction lie, if our stepchildren do not want to know us and we are also cold-shouldered by society? We tie ourselves in knots trying to resolve this issue. I hope that the following provides something of an answer.

The Primary Reward of Step-parenting

Becoming a step-parent is an unacknowledged rite of passage. It propels you into a demanding world where the everyday rules of give-and-take are distorted out of all recognition. We all have our own assumptions about what we deserve in terms of appreciation. Step-parenting turns these assumptions upside-down and inside-out. In the early days of step-parenthood, to give rarely means to receive.

We're right there, cooking meals, chauffeuring, shopping, reading bedtime stories, planning and funding holidays. And yet none of this seems to make an impression on our stepchildren. They have their own difficulties, which are often translated into scorn for their step-parent. Communicating gratitude is not high up on a stepchild's list of Things to Do Today.

So if, in the early days of stepfamily life, the reward does not come from your stepchildren, where does it come from? When the going gets tough, the core satisfaction comes from the same source as your stepfamily itself, which is your sexual relationship. For in doing a great job of looking after your partner's children, you're also doing a great job of looking after your partner. It's as simple as that. When thanks are not forthcoming from your stepchildren, you can take comfort in the knowledge that you are safeguarding something of enormous value: your partnership. Tweaking the usual rules of give-and-take is one way of minimising this extra pressure. Step-parents have to get used to giving in one direction and looking in quite another direction for endorsement.

Acquiring stepchildren puts most partnerships under great strain. The statistics are alarming: 25 per cent of stepfamilies break down in the first year. And within four years, this figure has risen to 44 per cent of remarriages failing. The unavoidable conclusion is that coping with stepchildren creates an additional pressure inside the home. The step dynamic does not have to be awash with touchy-feely sentimentality. Nor do you have to summon up instant love for these youngsters. But every step-parent must make sure that they do a good enough job that their primary relationship continues to flourish.

Enjoying life with your partner is just compensation for all that step-parenting graft. It's only by putting in the graft that you can enjoy life with your partner. Ultimately, if you don't try to make a go of things with your partner's children you will weaken the fabric of what holds you together as a couple. For biological parents are an insanely protective breed: if they perceive you as hostile to their kids, this will have an immediate and harmful effect.

None of us wants to end up as one of those stepfamily divorce statistics. In order to keep what we have, namely a strong partnership, we need to value this in itself as being our greatest possible reward. Rather than expecting torrents of gratitude from our stepchildren, we should learn to be grateful that our partnerships live and endure and get stronger by the day. It's a fine perk of the job.

The Secondary Reward of Step-parenting

When difficulties erupt with your stepchildren, it's important to hold on to the basic principle that pledging yourself to care for your stepchildren is an indirect way of looking after your own happiness. Valuing your partner means valuing your relationship with his or her children.

This reasoning should provide a little ballast when things are stormy. It can take a long time for stepfamilies to settle down. Getting used to the reality of living under one roof is usually a struggle. This is what psychologists call the 'phase of adjustment', which is generally believed to last at least two years. During this phase, everyone is feeling their way. Anger, aggression and rebellion get mixed up into a toxic combination. You may feel absolutely defeated, and on a regular basis too.

However when life is bleak inside your stepfamily, remember that things improve over time. It may seem implausible right now, but one day your stepchildren will appreciate your input. Chances are this will far exceed simple appreciation. In the future, your stepchildren will hold you in great affection. And this is of course the secondary reward of step-parenting.

Stepchildren can only thaw towards an unwanted step-parent when they are ready. It sure took a while in our household. Your stepchildren need to realise that they can trust you, and this is very much a long-term project. Until trust is established, all feedback is kept to a minimum. So do yourself a favour: don't expect too much from your stepchildren. They will come to you on their own terms. Until then, if at all possible, try to expect absolutely nothing. It's a great recipe for preserving everyone's sanity.

Making the Effort

All of us need motivation if we are to rise to the challenge of good step-parenting. Whatever motivates you, whether it's safeguarding your partnership or earning your stepchildren's trust and respect, we need to get our impetus from somewhere. For being a step-parent is a highly demanding business. It requires a massive effort of will.

A step-parent is absorbed into a pre-existing biological unit of parent and child, thus transforming that unit into a new entity that is your stepfamily. But nobody is entirely comfortable with the transformation. You now have to share your lover with his or her children from a previous relationship. And these same children have to reckon with a stranger who provokes jealousy.

And then there is the pivotal figure, the biological parent, caught in the middle and pulled in different directions by the mutually exclusive needs of lover and offspring. Both parties compete for the attention of this critical figure and rivalry takes hold. Unfortunately every stepfamily is a potential love triangle.

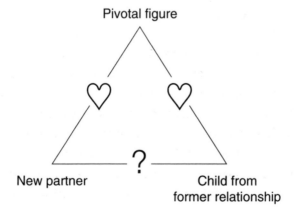

Pivotal figure

New partner

Child from
former relationship

The dangers of the love triangle are legendary. Nobody wants to share the object of their passion. Arguably, this happens to an extent inside any family, as children impact on a couple's ability to find time for each other. But the genetic link guarantees a degree of tolerance, a guarantee that is lacking in the stepfamily. A lover resents the demands of children not from his or her genetic stock. The children feel violently that this person is trespassing on their territory. The temperature rises as the conflict hardens. Each and everyone gives in to self-pity, not least the pivotal figure caught in the middle of warring factions.

The person with whom we fell in love witnesses our descent into a pit of childish reactions. For this is the reality of the step dynamic. It exposes the most needy side of our character. Where we were once rational, sussed, fun-loving individuals, the step dynamic works its black magic and we find ourselves reduced to frustrated, jealous monsters whom we hardly recognise. None of us likes to have our personal anxieties exposed in this way.

In researching this book, I interviewed numerous men and women who had direct experience of stepfamily life. Out of all these step-parents, only a tiny minority claimed that jealousy had never affected them. Most recognised an element of competition. Acknowledging this had been painful for some, as one stepfather explained:

> When we were just dating, Megan told me that it was all quite intense between her and her two kids. But nothing prepared me for when I moved in. Suddenly Megan was crazily straddling the gap between me and them. I was shocked by how deeply I resented the children. So many times, I just wished it could be just the two of us, just Megan and me on our own . . .

This is the mainspring of a step-parent's guilt. Wishing that your partner's children were out of the picture is not a reaction that inspires pride. We find ourselves in a quasi-parental role and yet cannot muster up anything like a parental response, which intensifies the guilt. We feel bad and this quickly slides into feeling angry at ourselves, at our stepchildren, even at our partner for not resolving the situation.

It's these dangerous emotions that a step-parent has to make the effort to overcome. The challenge is written into our daily lives: can we protect and consolidate our partnerships by trying to be a good enough step-parent? Are we going to rise to the challenge or sink into that pit of childish neediness? Is your stepfamily going to pull through or become yet another casualty statistic? You have a choice here, if you are prepared to turn a critical eye on what is going on inside your stepfamily.

The Critical Eye

Some people take to step-parenting like ducks to water. They have a natural capacity to stand back, keep cool and relish their detached status in their stepfamily. This fortunate few are free from the rivalry described above. They have a natural confidence and are perfectly able to let their partner get on with being a parent without feeling left out, hard-done-by or jealous. In short, these lucky individuals were born to be step-parents.

Most of us, however, get dragged down by the problems inherent in the triangular dynamics of our stepfamily. We need to get a grip on the step scenario. The only way that we can do this is by being tuned in to what's going on. This heightened level of awareness is the single most important tool for the harassed step-parent. Once you have made the decision to concentrate, all things become possible.

Many aspects of stepfamily life are beyond your control. You have walked into an atmosphere that is clouded by the fall-out from divorce or bereavement. Your partner, your stepchildren and the ex-spouse all have their pain and it sure makes itself felt. But there is one thing that you can control: yourself. Although you are only one of the players, resolving to focus on the quality of your input will have far-reaching consequences for everyone.

Think of your step-parenting life as a performance which needs to be constantly reviewed and modified. Just as an actor learns their lines, a step-parent has to learn the limits of their role. For most of us are not born to step-parent. Most of us make a lot of mistakes while we are trapped in the vertices of the love triangle. But with self-discipline, we can improve.

Making a Go of It

Much of our experience as a step-parent is predetermined: we are simply the latest addition to a drama that's already up and running. A couple have problems and then separate, or a parent dies and that leaves a space which you eventually come to occupy. How you are treated by your stepchildren, and even by your partner, is to a large extent dictated by what's gone before.

All separations are traumatic, but some heal better than others. Coming into a situation where the trauma is still fresh is likely to make your task much more difficult. The turmoil of the past continues to hold everyone in its grip, seeping into the present and taking over. Consequently you may be the only one in your stepfamily who's in a position to look to the future (for your partner's other role as mum or dad tends to dominate).

Although we might rail against all the negative assumptions, prejudices and aggro with which we are greeted, an incoming step-parent is uniquely placed to establish a new, positive unit which everyone will come to appreciate. Sure, we have to pick up the pieces of their lingering heartbreak. And yes, we have to bear the brunt of a whole lot of miscellaneous anger, but this is something we must learn to do if we are to survive.

All stepchildren have one thing in common, which is their loss.

Even those who never actually experienced their mother and father living together nurse a sense that they have been deprived of something important. When a single parent hitches up with someone new, this is a potential source of recovery. You are fixing something broken: taking one half of a couple and making it whole again.

It's important to remember what you bring to the table as a step-parent. All too often, we are made to feel less than welcome. But there are so many heartening stories out there of unhappy lives being coaxed back to happiness by a willing team of step-parent and parent. As the first cornerstone sets out, building a stepfamily really is a joint effort.

Believing in the future is half the battle. Parents are ambitious for their biological offspring, and we should be similarly ambitious for our stepfamilies. In the days of its infancy, this delicate creation needs a lot of nurturing. Just as parents are under an obligation to care for their newborn, we are under an obligation to care for our newly formed stepfamily. Just commit yourself to making things better, to improving on what you have, and it will happen, not overnight but over time. Be patient and you will be amazed at what you can build.

In the Beginning

Get together with a parent and it's only a matter of time until you will be introduced to his or her children. It's easy to feel daunted by the prospect of meeting the juniors. Apprehension is an understatement; most of us succumb to alarm. The pressure is on, both from ourselves and from our lover. 'Oh my kids will love you!' goes the cry.

But this is exactly what our stepchildren will not do, at least not any time soon. Love is out of the question, and yet most of us lean on this as the only appropriate model. Without our realising it, this becomes our secret hope. Consciously or subconsciously we believe we can only be accepted if we are loved. Instantly we have made our lives hell by longing for something that is a long, long way off. And in the mean time we are left with the acute awareness that we are unloved, which makes us feel rubbish.

We need to work on the rules of engagement here. Of course the situation is pressured. Because we are smitten with their mummy or daddy, we are desperate to make a favourable impression. But don't let the pressure get to you – this will only interfere with your ability to make a good impression. Remember that all you really need from these children is a degree of respect.

This is the crux of the step dynamic. Your stepchildren do *not* have to like you. Honestly, it's normal for a stepchild to declare to all and sundry that he hates your guts. And that is absolutely fine. You are not a failure if they don't like you. In fact, you may be on the road to success if you can wear their dislike lightly.

The only thing that you need is to be allowed to share your life with your new partner. As a couple, both of you may have to train your stepchildren into allowing you this basic minimum, and as a step-parent this is your only requirement. Let yourself believe that a hostile stepchild cannot damage what the two of you have. Talk it through with your partner, discuss your fears. You may worry about the effects of a hostile stepchild but it is highly likely that their mum or dad will simply shrug their shoulders.

So let's recalibrate our expectations. Go back to the primary reward of step-parenting discussed earlier. Provided that you are just about tolerated by your stepchildren, you can continue to enjoy your partnership. And sharing your life with this person is your principal benefit. As long as your stepchildren do not interfere with your personal happiness, let them get on with their stuff, whether it is angry sulking or downright loathing. All you ask for is a little space for the two of you to be adults together.

Ask your stepchildren to respect what you have as a couple, as they in turn ask you to respect what they have with their parent. These two relationships are so fundamentally different from each other that they do not bear comparison, and yet because both you and the stepchildren appear to want the same thing, namely the love of the pivotal figure, the comparisons begin. Who is loved more? Is it me or is it the kids?

This poisonous line of thought wreaks havoc. For there is no competition here. You win as lover; the kids win as kids. These two relationships are so profoundly distinct that conflict should not arise. Of course humans are nowhere near perfect and the competitive spirit rears its head. But we have to stamp out this false competition. There are two prizes here, not one. The love of a parent for his or her children ranks equally with the love of your partner for you. Just as you are not eligible for their prize, they are not eligible for your prize. You are not threatened by your stepchildren because you already have your reward. And now you can relax and enjoy the ride.

Keep this distinction clear in your mind and you will have cracked one of the mysteries of your new role. When both parties appreciate that the one doesn't mess with the other, trust takes root and you can take it from there.

You are much more likely to win the stepchildren round by sticking to your policy of detachment. By keeping your distance, you are making it clear that you've no intention of getting in the way of their relationship with their mum or dad. And this is the reassurance that all children need.

Many step-parents try way too hard. We are not used to the level of antipathy that we encounter, and find it upsetting, so we bend over backwards to be liked. Inadvertently, we alienate our stepchildren in the process. Children are proud creatures. They have their own fierce integrity which prevents them from befriending the enemy.

But a step-parent should not retreat entirely. The aim is to keep yourself outside their parent–child space. Their hostility is just a means of protecting that space. However there *is* a vacuum which can be colonised and that is your relationship with them.

Your stepchildren know nothing about you as an individual. They might be utterly convinced that their own reactions to you are based in reality. On the other hand, you are older and wiser and can see that their resistance is rooted in their own fears about what's going to happen to their time with Mum or Dad. So even when your stepchildren are wrapped up in their own negative attitude, remind yourself that one day they will come to see you for the person you are.

So, whilst keeping out of the zone that belongs exclusively to parent and child, you can also set about tentatively colonising the void that stretches between you and your stepchildren. Just because they don't want you to be their parent, it doesn't mean that they don't want anything at all from you. Ironically, they want you to be interested in them even if they rebuff your interest. They are not blind to the effort you put in as a step-parent, they are not deaf to praise, and compliments always hit home. Relax and have the confidence to make overtures on your own terms as a step-parent, not a parent.

Achieving Consensus

It's extraordinary that there's no status attached to step-parenting when we have so much to offer. In being furtive about our lives as step-parents, we are doing nothing to dismantle society's paranoia. Assumptions that all stepfamilies are fractured and unhappy are in need of correction. We should be proud of our input, for a step-parent can be:

- An extra source of love and support, both emotional and often financial

- A loyal supporter who can be straightforward in ways that a biological parent sometimes cannot
- A positive role model, setting a good example for the stepchildren
- An agent for recovery, in building a new partnership and mending a broken home

We need to abandon the traditional bias and stand up for ourselves. Yet many step-parents are reluctant to own up to the label, believing they are not enough of a practical 'mother' or 'father' to their stepchildren. This however is missing the point. Your identity as a step-parent has nothing to do with how many meals you've cooked or how much kiddie football you've played. Your identity as a step-parent is defined by your union with the mother or father of your stepchildren.

Instead of shaking off the mantle, wouldn't it be fantastic to feel proud of being a step-parent? The step-parenting role comes in many different shapes and sizes but every step-parent deserves recognition. It can be depressing being told that you're not a *real* step-parent because your stepchildren don't live with you full-time. This happens to me frequently and I always feel like yelling, 'What exactly am I to these girls, if *not* their step-mother?'

It is ironic that a society which places no value on the role of the step-parent simultaneously makes it as difficult as possible to qualify as one. The legal convention from the United Kingdom to the United States is that you are only a step-parent if the step-children are domiciled under your roof.

If the step-parenting community is going to foster a collective identity, we need to know who's in the collective. Are you a step-parent if your stepchildren are non-resident? The answer is undoubtedly yes: your partnership has endowed you with a tremendous power as far as your stepchildren are concerned. They may be leading their own lives and even have their own children, but this does not absolve you of your duty towards them. As long as you stick with their mother or father, your responsibility continues.

Consensus is necessary here. For the purposes of this book, I have devised a Step-parents' Charter to achieve just that.

The Step-parents' Charter

- You are a step-parent if you cohabit with someone who has children from a previous relationship
- Your identity as a step-parent is not defined by or dependent upon the amount of time that you spend looking after your stepchildren. It is irrelevant whether they live with you or not
- You are a step-parent regardless of the age of your stepchildren. Adults do not stop needing the emotional support of their parents
- As step-parents we accept that we have a responsibility to our partner to try to make the best relationship we can with our stepchildren
- Our partners are under a reciprocal responsibility to support us in our role as step-parents, because we will need all the support we can get
- Step-parents have a valuable contribution to make and deserve recognition for their positive input

The Benefits of Making It Work

If you let yourself be defeated by what is dished up inside your stepfamily, it's not just you who suffers but your partner too. As one authority stated, 'The quality of the stepparent–stepchild relationship [is] a strong predictor of marital quality.'[1]

Thus the dynamic between step-parent and stepchild goes to

the very heart of every stepfamily. Kay Pasley, one of the leading authorities on stepfamily relations, has shown that the nature of the step-tie dictates the level of stress within the household.

Managing the separate interests contained within a stepfamily is the classic balancing act. It's like walking the tightrope, where your needs must not outweigh the needs of your stepchildren. Your requirements do not come second but they do not come first either.

For now, enjoy what you do have, which is your relationship. And don't fret about what you don't have, which is the undying love of your stepchildren. Pace yourself for what lies ahead and one day your stepchildren will include you among their band of core supporters. This is one dream that you can realise, if you have the determination, honesty and courage to rise to the challenge of step-parenting.

2

Self-Assessment Questionnaire

As step-parents, we all have areas in which we function well, whilst other areas do not bring out the best in us. We know that our ability to cope fluctuates and that certain aspects of step-family life trigger tension. And yet the process of identifying these strengths and weaknesses is made harder by the blanket of social expectations pressurising us to keep such difficulties to ourselves.

Shaking off this blanket and owning up to whatever issues are particularly problematic for you personally is the only way that anybody can hope to progress and improve on what they have to offer as a step-parent. As Thomas Dewar said, 'Minds are like parachutes, they operate only when open.'[1] Although this is not a highly complex psychometric, your answers to the following questions will establish where you are succeeding and where you are dropping the ball as a step-parent.

Each question focuses on a single statement. What you have to decide is how accurately this statement reflects your attitude. Use the following sliding scale to grade your response and circle the appropriate number for each question.

This is 100% accurate	1
This is often true	2
This is occasionally true	3
This is rarely the case	4
This is never the case	5

1. My partner will *not* tolerate my stepchild(ren) being rude to me   1 2 3 4 5

2. I don't need to prove myself to my stepchild(ren)   1 2 3 4 5

3. I know that much of the aggro in my stepfamily has nothing to to do with me   1 2 3 4 5

4. My stepchild(ren) value(s) me as a source of friendship   1 2 3 4 5

5. Talking to my partner about my relationship with my stepchild(ren) is always helpful   1 2 3 4 5

6. I'm comfortable with my stepchild(ren)'s reactions to me   1 2 3 4 5

7. After a row with my stepchild(ren), I find it easy enough to forgive and forget   1 2 3 4 5

8. I make an effort not to be rude about my partner's ex in front of my stepchild(ren)   1 2 3 4 5

9. I used to feel excluded around my stepchild(ren), but I don't so much any more   1 2 3 4 5

10. I know that I am also responsible for my stepchild(ren)'s welfare   1 2 3 4 5

11. My stepchild(ren) does/do not have the power to threaten or undermine my relationship with my partner   1 2 3 4 5

12. Praising my stepchild(ren) comes naturally　　1 2 3 4 5

13. My partner understands that being a
    step-parent can be tricky　　1 2 3 4 5

14. Generally, I don't mind playing second fiddle　　1 2 3 4 5

15. When I feel frustrated with the situation, I
    know how to calm myself down　　1 2 3 4 5

16. I am involved in and hopeful about my
    stepchild(ren)'s future　　1 2 3 4 5

17. My partner and I broadly agree in our
    attitudes towards the stepchild(ren)　　1 2 3 4 5

18. I'm satisfied with the feedback I get from
    my stepchild(ren)　　1 2 3 4 5

19. Paranoia is not something I feel around my
    stepchild(ren)　　1 2 3 4 5

20. I am proud of my relationship with my
    stepchild(ren)　　1 2 3 4 5

The scoring breaks down the questions into four groups, corresponding to the four cornerstones, an approach that will become familiar to you over the following chapters.

Use the table below to list your answers for each of the questions included in Group 1, before adding these together to get your total for that category. Read the analysis of your score and then complete the subsequent tables.

Group 1: The First Cornerstone

Your total for questions 1, 5, 9, 13 and 17: ☐

If your score was 0–15:   Your experience of stepfamily life exposes such raw emotions as jealousy and isolation. This sense of being on the sidelines indicates that you do not feel fully supported by your partner.

If your score was 16–25:   This suggests that you are already moving towards being an integrated member of your stepfamily. You manage to keep feelings of exclusion under control and work well with your partner.

Group 2: The Second Cornerstone

Your total for questions 2, 6, 10, 14 and 18: ☐

If your score was 0–15:   You can be threatened by the axis that unites your partner to his/her child. You are locked into a painful struggle to keep up, push forward and be heard, and find it hard to relax into stepfamily life.

If your score was 16–25:   You are reconciled to the limited nature of your role as a step-parent. You are not trying to prove yourself either to your partner or to your stepchild(ren) and are relatively easy-going.

Group 3: The Third Cornerstone

Your total for questions 3, 7, 11, 15 and 19: ☐

If your score was 0–15:   It doesn't take much for your stepchild(ren) to press your buttons. You have been known to overreact and sometimes have difficulty seeing things in context.

If your score was 16–25:   Keeping a sense of perspective comes naturally to you. It's vital for a step-parent to be able to detach and this is one skill that you already possess.

Group 4: The Fourth Cornerstone

Your total for questions 4, 8, 16 and 20: ☐

If your score was 0–15:   Past hostility and unresolved issues have taken their toll on your relationship with your stepchild(ren). At present you lack the confidence to be giving.

If your score was 16–25:   You take pleasure in expressing your positive feelings for your stepchild(ren) and know that you have much to offer. You are sure of the value of what you can give and what you can be for your partner's child(ren).

The above analysis should flag up areas of particular concern for you and help direct you to the relevant sections of this book. Map out your own course, starting with whichever cornerstone you think is of most relevance. Although these four principles can be dismantled into separate points, it's worth mentioning that the best results are achieved when the cornerstones are fused together into a single, unified approach. Before you get down to work, remember that we start from the same baseline, which applies equally to all of us. To do our job well, we need confidence and this is the subject of the next chapter.

3

The Confidence Trick

If there is a single defining feature of the step-parent, it is self-doubt. We ask ourselves endless questions, query our right to be absorbed into an existing family unit, and rake over what is said and not said. Did we handle that OK? Should we have handled it differently?

The purpose of this book is to give you confidence as a stepmother or stepfather. As described by the husband-and-wife team of psychologists Emily and John Visher, 'There are so many moving parts to a stepfamily that it is more open to conflicts than the usual family. The major task is to develop some feeling of wholeness.'[1]

We all perform better when are sure of what we are doing, whether at work or at play. But this is the central problem about being a step-parent: getting to know the ropes is a lonely business.

There is no general understanding of the step-parenting basics. And there are no shallow waters in which to dabble. One minute you are Joe or Joanna Normal, the next you've transmogrified into Joe the stepdad or Joanna the stepmum. Becoming a step-parent has the capacity to be a life-changing experience, right up there alongside natural parenthood. Everyone knows what's expected of a good parent – but what do we expect of an outsider coming into an existing family unit? Are we meant to be doing our own thing here or not?

Step-parents provide something that is quite their own. We just need to have enough confidence to break away from the mother/father model, to do our own thing, to build up a support network that endorses our contribution and calms self-doubt.

Drawing Up the Agenda

It's one of those awkward truths that being a step-parent comes with no job description. This results in a haphazard process of trial and error, with the new arrival setting his or her own standards, which are usually impossible to achieve. We want so badly to succeed that we write our own job descriptions which are hopelessly over the top and way too ambitious.

This kind of unrealistic approach blights many a step-parent. Research has shown that step-parents tend to blame themselves whenever problems arise at home.[2] On some level, we feel guilty about our appearance on the scene.

We all recognise, either consciously or subconsciously, that having a step-parent is a complicating factor in the life of any child. Immediately this puts us on the defensive. Although our partner wants us around, our stepchildren are ambivalent at best, and such ambivalence feeds into our own anxieties about our new identity.

We need to draw up an agenda here for maintaining our self-esteem. We want to feel buoyant despite the unfamiliarity of the step dynamic. The key is to acknowledge some of the damaging emotions that prevent a step-parent from relaxing into his or her new role. For when we are relaxed we are confident. It's time to examine some of the dark forces that can eat into a step-parent's peace of mind. For we can only be truly confident when we know what we are up against.

Avoiding the Pitfalls

Because the stepfamily appears to be the classic love triangle, it's all too easy to let jealousy take hold. And because we try hard to make a go of things, we really mind when our efforts are not appreciated. We feel taken for granted and this crystallises into resentment or, worse still, depression and a sense of failure.

And yet we have not actually done anything wrong and curse the injustice of being made into the scapegoat. Anger takes hold as we are blamed for much that is not our fault. We feel angry towards our stepchildren and this instantly provokes self-doubt: how can we be angry with innocent youngsters? We feel guilt that we do not feel more affection. We are envious of their unconditional love for our partner and wish that we were equally loved, which brings us full circle. And so the cycle goes on reverberating between jealousy, resentment, anger and guilt.

Breaking this cycle of negativity is more than possible. For each step-parenting vice has a solution that is defined in one of the four cornerstones.

1. Jealousy

A step-parent is by definition outside the family group which he or she joins. We are excluded from the absolute link between parent and child. We are also excluded from their past, the accumulated years of shared laughter and memories.

In the beginning, we are fully aware that we are entering the private domain of their family. We are reluctant to trespass on territory that does not belong to us, and try to keep our distance. In other words, we begin full of sensible good intentions. However, this rarely lasts.

The rational approach with which we set sail quickly weakens, and before we realise what is going on, we have changed into someone who really minds being left out. It is a classic situation that taps into our earliest childhood experiences. The mere fact that something is inaccessible can make us long for access. It's human nature to want things that we cannot have; this impulse is built into our psyche, giving us purpose, ambition and drive. Unfortunately, it also gives us a lot of heartache. For, like it or not, most step-parents crave inclusion into an élite club of blood relatives.

Sometimes, we're not even sure what we are jealous of: is it the time that our partner spends with his or her children? Or is the attention, the love heaped on their young heads? Or is it the two-way street of all they share, the in-jokes, the secret language? Are we jealous of just how much our stepchildren love their mum or dad, our partner, because this is such a strong contrast with what they feel for us? We may not know what we want, but all we do know is that we don't have it and that really, really hurts.

Whatever causes the twinges, something sure as hell is eroding our former peace of mind. Where we were once cool, calm and collected, we now feel anxious and lonely – a frequent, inevitable complaint that goes with the turf. Ironically, and often without realising it, we shut out the one person who introduced us to stepfamily life, internalising our troubles rather than confessing to these dark emotions. Isolation makes us into forlorn, self-pitying creatures.

Self-pity is the last thing that a step-parent should give in to because we have one formidable asset: a strong partnership. At the risk of sounding trite, there are hundreds of thousands of single people out there who would dearly love to be in a valid, secure relationship with the right person. You've already found the right person and that is something to inspire deep gratitude.

If you and your partner choose to focus on what the two of you have, then those days of lonely exclusion will be over.

The first cornerstone – YOU AND YOUR PARTNER ARE A TEAM – brings this principle to life. It gives you the confidence to know what the two of you can be if you work together. Liberate yourself from any trace of rivalry; it's more than possible if you look in the right direction.

2. Resentment

Resentment is the carbon monoxide of stepfamily life: it is truly poisonous, killing off any tiny threads of affection. For step-parenting, like natural parenting, means work. In fact it means a lot of work. It's our mindset here that is the problem. We concentrate solely on the negative, on what we do not receive in the way of thanks and appreciation, which leaves us smarting, bitter and above all resentful.

We wish that we didn't count the cost, envying a biological mother or father's capacity to work tirelessly on behalf of his or her offspring, whilst we on the other hand are painfully aware of the labour we put in. We cannot push ourselves into caring autopilot, cruising along, nurturing and feeding and cleaning in a warm haze of selfless parental giving.

Counting the cost seems to be woven into the fabric of step-parenthood, but it is a terrible, poisonous vice that starves your stepfamily of oxygen. Endlessly monitoring of what isn't coming your way is soul-destroying. We expect praise that does not come and long for gratitude that is never expressed. We are left like children ourselves, with our hands outstretched, waiting . . .

Resentment is also rooted in what we do not have: the capacity to give that unites parent and child. For a natural parent does not stint in the care that he or she provides to a child, who is equally unstinting in the depth of his or her love for Mummy or Daddy. Without realising it, we compare ourselves to our partner in terms of both the freedom with which they give and the rewards they receive. We do not come off well on either score and our resentment intensifies.

We begin to ask ourselves what we are doing wrong, how we could improve our relationship with our stepchildren. So we launch into trying even harder to make an impression, bending over backwards to be helpful and accommodating. But still our efforts go unnoticed, or so it seems. We begin to wonder if things will ever change, if anything we do will ever be recognised.

Low self-esteem is one of the classic afflictions of step-parenthood. We all need acknowledgement for our labours, whether emotional or financial: without it, our sense of worth deflates into nothing.

A natural parent is emotionally remunerated by the relationship with his or her children but for a step-parent all the usual rules that govern social exchange are suspended.

Out in the real world there is a strict correlation between give and take. You put in hours at the office and receive a pay packet. You put in time with your friends and can rely on their friendship. You collect your kids from school and know that they think you're fantastic. But in the context of your stepfamily, you put in hours of manpower and are left wondering why you even bothered, since it feels as if you get nothing back.

As adults, we thought we understood the basics of social interaction. And yet suddenly these basics do not apply. Confusion is not something we want to feel in our own homes, so we fight back, convincing ourselves that if we shout we will be heard.

This is the origin of the step-parenting bully, an awful phenomenon enshrined in folklore. Like the school bully who covers up a sense of personal inadequacy with tough talk and fisticuffs, the domineering stepfather or stepmother seeks to regain control of a situation in which he or she feels out of control. For when a step-parent cannot command the affection of the stepchildren, he or she seeks to command authority as some small consolation.

Resentment, low self-esteem and domineering behaviour are all products of the same painful awareness that we are not getting what we expected. Bringing these expectations into line is what every step-parent has to do. This truth dawned on me slowly. I realised that, to my stepdaughters, I was very much a second-class citizen. But far from being a depressing moment, I felt absolutely liberated. Instead of wanting to be loved as much as their daddy, it was suddenly possible to accept my lot and get on with life as their stepmother. Instead of wanting more, I was quite happy with less.

The second cornerstone – KNOW YOUR ROLE – establishes a distinct model of behaviour that is appropriate to us and to what we do as step-parents. It puts an end to the unhappy comparison with our partners who are thriving as mothers and fathers, adored and idealised. This comparison makes us nothing but anxious because to our stepchildren we come a poor second. But this is just a fact, not an injustice. Accepting this fact is at the heart of good step-parenting. We need to have the confidence to realise what we cannot be, which is natural parents.

3. Rejection

Becoming a step-parent means upheaval. Your stepchildren, your partner and his or her ex-partner are all affected by your appearance on the scene. And if you have your own children, they too will be thrown by their new circumstances, as will your former spouse. Add the grandparents and watch another generation trying to adapt.

Tension levels run high at the shock of the new. All that was safe and normal has gone and been replaced by a weird, unknown construct. The stepchildren are the first to rebel. What they used to have with their parent has been taken from them – or so they fear. Their anger is obvious and free-floating until it latches on to you, the target. For you have brought about change.

Human nature is rigged up to protect what we know, the

secure territory of home. But the advent of a step-parent changes all that, stirring up comfortable, settled patterns, making waves, causing disturbance. The introduction of this new personality alters the climate which can be confusing for a child, as this step-son related to me:

> If you're in a family, you all know how to rub along together, until something changes. It's like a dance, one of those set routines like a Scottish reel where everyone knows what to do when. But then something changes, someone leaves, someone new joins in the dance, and you have to start all over again learning a new routine that fits the new group.
>
> The truth is that each family has their own dance, which has its own character. I learned this young, after my parents got divorced. I was about five and suddenly everything was different. In my mum's house, I was always funny. I could tell a joke and everyone would laugh. But not in my father's house, where he lived with his second wife. I don't think it was me inventing a different character, it's just that I was perceived in a different way. It was very strange to me, throughout my childhood: how could I be funny in this house and not funny in that house?

As the above case history demonstrates, a child's world is often turned upside-down by the arrival of a step-parent. Their family space has been modified to make way for someone who is frequently seen as an intruder. In self-defence a stepchild hits back, out to hurt because they are already hurt.

On the receiving end of their attacks, all a step-parent feels is the injustice of it all. He or she has done nothing wrong, and out in the real world, attacks on an innocent victim do not go unpunished, but once again these conventions cannot be translated into the stepfamily situation. You cannot rail against little Johnnie for stamping his foot and screaming that he hates you and wants Mummy. You know that he's just a child and cannot be blamed for his childish responses. Why then are you so upset? How does little Johnnie manage to stamp all over your well-being, making you sad, depressed or irritable?

We need to be armour-plated to withstand such personal assaults. A step-parent needs a tough hide. Consciously or not, the stepchildren want you to pay the price for ruining their fun.

And we do pay the price, because we suffer in knowing that we are not wanted. This taps into our early-childhood terror about being unloved. Here in the sanctuary of our own homes we are scorned by the children of the person we love; does this mean our partner will abandon us too? For our stepchildren have certainly abandoned us, discarding what we offer them and querying our hopes of a happy future in the process.

It's hard to contain such disappointment. Spurned and aggrieved, it becomes a struggle not to retaliate in kind. Like children in the school playground, pushing when they are pushed and kicking when they are kicked, the impulse is to fight back, to defend ourselves. But if we do fight back the antagonism intensifies, and a sense of shame develops that we cannot be more adult. Why does their aggression have the power to reduce us to this feeble playground kid who can only treat like with like?

I wrestled with this for an eternity, or so it felt. The hostility of my stepdaughters ate into my capacity to keep calm. I was tense, choked by self-pity. And I became deeply paranoid, so paranoid that I didn't even notice the mellowing of my stepdaughters towards me.

The third cornerstone – KEEP REJECTION AT ARM'S LENGTH – short-circuits this unnecessary angst. It provides a coping mechanism that frees you up from a destructive line of thought. We need to cut loose from all that erodes our confidence. A good step-parent knows when not to take it personally.

4. Guilt

Most step-parents suffer from the nagging doubts that they could be doing better. Deeply critical of the people we become around our stepchildren, we long to feel comfortable with ourselves as step-parents. But how can we be comfortable when the demons described above have us in their grip? Walking tall is not possible when we are consumed with lonely longing, obsessed with the idea that we've been not only hard-done-by but ill-treated too.

Becoming a step-parent often strains our self-image. Once upon a time, I used to think that I was a warm, generous person. Then I became a stepmother. Quite frankly, those early years left me feeling like a walking cesspit. So much for being the good guy. I was treated like the villain and to a degree that's what I became. And of course this provokes enormous guilt.

In acting out the villain, I was letting everyone down: my stepchildren, my partner and my own children. This hit home one day, when my four-year-old son shared a poignant confidence with me. In a solemn, almost protective voice, he informed me that although his big sister didn't like me, *he* did. Clearly it was difficult for such a young child to digest that his mother was not universally lovable. At an age when a mummy tends to be blissfully idealised, my son had to reckon with the fact that his half-sister didn't like me at all.

The truth dawned that I was a big disappointment to everyone, not least myself. We all want to avoid the cliché of the malevolent step-parent, nursing a sour, rancid attitude towards the stepchildren. And yet it's unbelievably hard to be likeable when you know you are disliked. Unfortunately, pain brings out the worst in all of us.

Our regrets however can be traced back to the lack of any received wisdom as to what a step-parent should and should not do. Because there is no step-parenting infrastructure, each of us is left to fathom it out for ourselves. On the one hand there is the biological model, but this makes us feel even more guilty. Next to the shining unconditional love of a mother or a father, our persona darkens still further.

However, if we use the right model, we can feel good about ourselves. This is what the first three cornerstones seek to establish. Sorting out an appropriate mindset where jealousy, resentment and rejection have been curtailed will effectively eradicate guilt. Securing your own agenda frees you up to be both detached and giving towards your stepchildren.

Confidence is what it is all about. We need confidence in our partnership to insulate us from jealousy. It takes real confidence to be at peace with our marginalised status as second-class citizens and not to expect too much from our stepchildren. And confidence is what enables us to shrug off hostility. Empowered in this way to stand back from the complicated dynamics of your stepfamily, you can then set about creating a sound relationship with your stepchildren.

The development of trust is a great turning point. To return to the analogy of the love triangle, in creating a proper, stable bond with your stepchildren you are correcting an imbalance. Before, all that you had in common with your stepchildren was your link to the pivotal figure. Now, however, you are building a bond that provides a direct link.

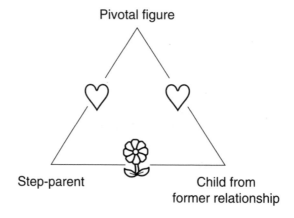

Pivotal figure

Step-parent

Child from
former relationship

This is the emphasis of the fourth and final cornerstone: YOUR STEPCHILDREN NEED YOUR LOVE. Allowing yourself to be warm and friendly is amazingly healing for everyone, soothing away all guilt at previous bad conduct. Dedicating yourself to being something positive in the lives of your stepchildren will bring stability to your stepfamily.

Even when antagonism has frozen all good will, it's remarkable how far a few carefully planned gestures, a casual compliment and a little praise go towards solving intractable difficulties. In a frosty atmosphere, summoning up the courage to break the ice and actually start being friendly takes confidence. However by keeping your mind's eye on each of the four cornerstones, you'll be able to drum up the necessary confidence and move towards a better future.

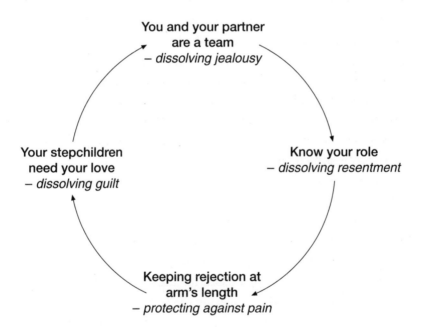

You and your partner
are a team
– *dissolving jealousy*

Know your role
– *dissolving resentment*

Your stepchildren
need your love
– *dissolving guilt*

Keeping rejection at
arm's length
– *protecting against pain*

Planning Ahead

Present conflict puts our faith in future happiness under strain. All stepfamilies have to go through this stressful period of adjustment that takes its toll on everyone. There are however two invaluable ways of linking current turmoil to the distant prospect of your ideal. Both are straightforward, and yet, when the going gets tough, they are easily forgotten. The first is communication, the second a belief in the future. Let's keep them firmly in mind.

Communication

There is no disputing the fact that, when tension levels rise, communication levels plummet. When we are in the grip of any of the vices outlined above, the reflex is to internalise our feelings because we at once are alarmed by and ashamed of them. The proud do not want to appear weak. And none of us wants to be mean. So we keep quiet, hoping that the bad stuff will pass.

Enduring a grim self-imposed silence is to give up on your stepfamily. But this newborn needs lots of attention and care. Just because things are difficult for you, this does not entitle you to shut down. You are under an obligation to your partner to reveal the ways in which you are struggling. Our partners are not mind readers: they can only help us once they are empowered with knowledge of what we are going through.

There is however another equally important axis of communication: what you choose to communicate to your stepchildren. This is another fraught area, for often it feels like the stepchildren are the source of the problem. Our feelings are so extreme that we dare not broach the subject, fearing the consequences. We're fully aware of the strength of their feelings. They do not trust us. And frequently they do not even want to hear what we have to say.

Many step-parents are intimidated by such intense hostility. We do not have the nerve to speak up because we know that our stepchildren are simply not interested. To them, we are scum; but does that mean we should give up?

Without communication, a stepfamily will never function as a family. First marriages can rely on years of accumulated non-verbal communication which minimises the need for a huge amount of discussion. From infancy, a child grows up in an atmosphere which is full of soothingly familiar faces, sounds, voices. The physical rapport that develops between a natural parent and a child is without analogy.

However, the majority of us begin our lives as step-parents when this early formative stage is long past. In the absence of these strong foundations, we have no option but to make up for lost time. The importance of disclosure was recognised in a paper given by Linda Thompson in her study 'Women and Men in Marriage, Work and Parenthood'.[3] We have to communicate if we are to establish any kind of trust.

There are a few ground rules here. Because your relationship with your stepchildren is a slender sapling, not a strong oak, you must take care. Communicating only becomes a positive if you weed out all that is impulsive, selfish and destructive. Sometimes all we want is to say it like it is and hurl insults because we get insulted. We want to give as good as we get and make it quite clear that we know where the blame lies.

But no one is to blame for the turbulence of your stepfamily. It is the situation that is turbulent. Young stepchildren cannot rationalise away their conviction that their step-parent is responsible for all their woes. But as the adult, you know that the stepchildren are not creating havoc by themselves. Just as you feel much more normal when your stepchildren are not present, these youngsters also have another life as unbothered kids when they're not around you.

Talking only works if it takes place in a neutral territory. You have to mark out this territory by concentrating hard on what you choose to say and how you choose to say it to your stepchildren.

Rule 1. *Always avoid the counter-attack.* No matter what is said or done, you must not sink to the level of mud-slinging. Even when seething, bite your tongue. Remember you're out to create trust, not make enemies. All of us have to lead by example.

Rule 2. *Owning up.* When conflict erupts it's only natural that you are left licking your wounds. There is however value in just admitting that you're finding things difficult. It's all too easy for your stepchildren not to see the person behind the step-parent mask. Sometimes it actually helps to draw attention to your condition.

You're not asking for sympathy here, but you are asking for a little recognition that you are human too. For their own reasons, stepchildren often want to close their eyes to this hidden truth. They actively want you to be the baddie. In telling them that you are upset, sad or having trouble, you are forcing them to acknowledge that you may not be all bad. All you are doing is asking them to reconsider their evaluation of you as someone who doesn't care.

Rule 3. *Keep it calm.* Dialogue is only constructive if it has no sting. If you're wound up, keep your mouth shut unless you are alone with your partner. And when the two of you are alone, make sure that everyone else is out of earshot before you let rip. I remember one terrible time when I was letting off steam to my husband and my stepdaughters overheard. The aftershock continued for months.

As a rule of thumb, if you feel that there's the slightest chance that you are going to explode, then steer clear of jeopardising your relationship with your stepchildren. Take your troubles elsewhere until you've got them in perspective.

Rule 4. *Avoid blame.* Stepchildren do not tolerate being criticised by their step-parent. The incipient relationship is simply not strong enough to take the strain, so don't risk it. Even after years and years on the scene, the wise step-parent never indulges the urge to have a go. Holding your stepchildren responsible for the way you feel amounts to a criticism; *'You* are hurting my feelings . . .' is pointing an accusatory finger. On the other hand, calmly informing them that 'Actually I feel a hurt by what's been said' is a more acceptable, less aggressive way of saying the same thing.

A stepchild will feel antagonised if they are accused of causing your malaise. Keep it neutral. 'It's a shame because I spent all afternoon researching this' is much more acceptable than *'You* don't know how long it took me to find out about this! *You* have no idea how many hours I spent browsing the web for this information! *You* are so ungrateful!' Removing the second-person from your forms of address can be hard. Yet it's a habit that's well worth acquiring.

Rule 5. *Be reassuring.* Much of the aggro that we experience stems from our stepchildren's fear that we are going to obstruct their relationship with their mum or dad. A little clarity from you here will go a long way. Don't be coy about telling your stepchildren that you know your place and it certainly isn't to come between them and their parent. Openly state your agenda. Explain your role as a step-parent in a way that will calm them down and avoid doubt. 'Look, Johnnie, I know you don't like me and that's OK. But I think you're a great kid who needs his dad . . .' Dismantle their fears: nobody is stealing anybody away.

All families have run-ins and tidying them up afterwards is productive for everyone. Apologising where necessary and accepting responsibility are all part of the process. We want our stepchildren to grow up feeling that it's normal to have the odd argument, not that they are big scary things which never die. In rowing and making up we are demonstrating our commitment to our stepchildren. And by the by we are also fostering trust.

Rule 6. *Positive feedback.* The times when you feel quite unable to be nice to anyone are exactly the times when you should force yourself to do just that. We all know that if you're mired in tension, simply laughing provides relief. And the same applies to a house full of bad vibes: a bit of positive feedback clears the air.

I'm not advocating that you whisk up a completely new personality for yourself. The stepchildren have to come to terms with the real you, not some dummy dishing out phoney remarks and cheesy grins. But there is a middle way between icy silence and patronising schmaltz.

There is something about the step dynamic that dupes a step-parent into treating their stepchildren almost like mini-adults. Unwittingly, we leave an important factor out of the equation, which is their extreme youth. They are tentatively beginning to find their way in the world and it's an anxious business. Take a second to recall your uncertainties at their stage of life. Young people need an enormous amount of nurturing attention. This is such an obviously helpful thing that you can do for them and there's no reason on earth not to do it.

Whatever you say, no matter how inconsequential, your stepchildren will on some level be grateful. Of all the stepchildren that I interviewed, many felt unsupported by their step-parent. One stepdaughter, now a mother herself, told me:

My stepfather always kept his distance emotionally. He came to live with us when I was thirteen, and in one way I was incredibly relieved because suddenly there was someone to look after my mum. However, he just stayed separate. I knew he had high standards, but I never felt that I was meeting them.

He disapproved of me so badly. At least that's how it felt to me. But now, with hindsight, I realise that I was reading too much into his silence. He did disapprove a bit, but not nearly as much as I thought he did. It was a shame really.

I had this mental block that stopped us from getting to know each other. That didn't really happen until I was grown-up, in my mid-twenties. Now I can see all his good qualities, what he did for us, putting me and my brothers through private education and everything. He's a very kind man, but he just didn't let me know that at the time . . .

This stepfather did nothing to dispel his stepdaughter's firm belief that she didn't make the grade. She wanted approval and none was forthcoming. Much heartache could have been avoided if a little encouragement had come her way.

Practical Exercise

There are a number of these exercises dotted through the following chapters, designed to project the issues discussed on to your personal situation. In order to get the most out of these exercises, get hold of a plain, school-type notebook. This is to become your Step-parenting Record, a private document that charts your progress.

The first task is to focus on your communication skills with your stepchildren:

1. Go through the six rules of communication above
2. Ask yourself how well you do in each category. Give yourself a score out of ten in the following areas, and be honest:

   Always avoid the counter-attack   Avoid blame

   Owning up   Be reassuring

   Keep it calm   Positive feedback
3. Which rule do you find easiest to follow?
4. Conversely, which one causes you the most problems?
5. Focus on ways in which you can strengthen your communication skills

Believing in the Future

What starts off as an unhappy step dynamic will almost always improve over the years. Stories of domestic transformation occurred time and again in interviews, mirroring my own experience. We were in danger but then we weathered the storm.

Contrary to popular belief, most stepfamilies do weather the storm.

If you are currently in the throes of a tempestuous dynamic, the idea that the nightmare will pass can seem laughable, downright unbelievable. But pessimism on this scale prolongs the nightmare; waking up to a better future will only happen if you start to believe in such a future. Regardless of what's going on in your stepfamily, you have to keep the faith that one day things will be much, much better.

In order to commit to any kind of work, we need to know what we hope to achieve at the end of it all. Objectives make us focus. They give us endurance and provide stamina when we are flagging. Without a clear understanding of the goals we are aiming for, we are much more likely to quit. But quitting is one thing that we cannot do in the context of our stepfamily. We need the situation to improve, but it's only going to improve if we know what we're working towards. In other words we have to imagine ourselves as part of a happier scene, and we have to hold on to that thought, to give us purpose and direction.

Practical Exercise

Open up your Step-parenting Record and write a heading: 'The Best is Yet to Come'.

1. Let yourself imagine the rosiest picture possible of your stepfamily, where you are all getting along well, accepting each other with ease. Put your inhibitions on one side, and write down some of these hopes

2. Can you let yourself believe in such a positive picture? Is something holding you back from committing to a happier future?

3. What is holding you back? You have a choice here. Are you going to stick with your negative approach or take the plunge and go for the unknown option, a future that is friendly, not fraught?

Turning around a dysfunctional stepfamily is a highly demanding challenge. You'll need all the stamina you can summon. Having a sharp image in your mind's eye of future good times helps smooth over current difficulties. By forcing yourself to remember times that you've all enjoyed together, you are thinking constructively instead of destructively. If all is doom and gloom today, offset present negativity with a little hope. It's a surprisingly potent commodity.

Here are some ways of crystallising your hopes:

1. *Affirmations*. At the end of a gruelling day, we can all feel beaten up by our experiences as a step-parent. Affirmations help to restore your sense of worth. These are bald statements that correct a warped perception that you are failing, e.g. 'I am a great person and a good step-parent.' Sometimes it helps to concentrate directly on your stepchildren – 'Little Johnnie is a great kid'; 'I love little Madeleine.'

The above may sound corny but it just opens up your mind to other possibilities. In telling yourself that you are a loving step-mum or stepdad, you are allowing yourself the luxury of becoming such a thing.

2. *Consolidating the past*. You've completed your first innings with your stepfamily. Probably, amidst the exhaustion, you had a few glimmers of fun. Just reminiscing about funny incidents, retelling favourite jokes and sharing fond memories are all beneficial, healthy ways of tying up lose ends.

Sometimes these good times were caught on camera. Watching fuzzy old videos of everyone at their best and worst makes it clear that from the outside at least you look like one big happy stepfamily.

Reliving past moments that you all shared is a great experience. Going through old photos of holidays, or having a group photo framed, are means of communicating a subtle message about the strength and importance of your stepfamily.

Practical Exercise

Take a stroll through your home and make a note of any and every way in which you personally have acknowledged your stepchild's presence. In other words, what have you done to demonstrate to your stepchild that you care?

1. Are there any photographs up of you and your stepchild?
2. Is it plain for all to see that you value a present that they may have given you, or endorse their achievements by displaying their school certificates of merit, or one of their artworks?

3. Hatching plans. This is another way of demonstrating your commitment to your life with your stepchildren. Involving them in discussions about what you're going to do, whether it's this Saturday or the destination for your next holiday, is sending a message that you value your time with them and put energy into devising fun stuff.

Youngsters love to be involved like this. In asking them what they like and don't like, you are giving them status as well as hinting at future fun. Having things to look forward to is good for everyone's spirits.

Optimism is a quality of fundamental importance when it comes to your stepfamily. Your optimism is not misplaced; it simply reflects the statistical likelihood that things will improve. So have the confidence to let your hopes take root.

Use the four cornerstones to map out a route that makes you feel sure-footed and secure. Nothing is insurmountable if you step-parent with care.

4

The First Cornerstone:
You and Your Partner Are a Team

Meet your new partner's children for the first time and you are instantly aware of an awkward truth: that you are in a minority of one and the blood relatives are in the majority of two or more. The stepchildren are not looking for anyone else to swell the numbers. We are left wondering how to relate when we are not a relation.

The American writer Delia Ephron neatly summed up the conundrum:

> Lisa and Alex, ages six and three, were standing in a fountain in the middle of the Santa Monica Mall. I insisted they get out. They refused. Again I insisted. Lisa put her arm around her brother and drew him closer to her.
>
> This is what happened the first time I was left alone with my future stepchildren. I insisted they get out of a fountain that did not have water in it. I have given this act of mine considerable thought. At the very least, it indicates a certain amount of panic on my part. A tendency to overreact. Certainly a lack of playfulness. I could have gotten into the fountain with them. I also could have

ignored the whole business, waited for their father to return, and let him deal with it or not. But I couldn't wait. I had to seize an opportunity, any opportunity, to assert my authority.

My claim to authority at that time was tenuous – I was not yet their stepmother. I must have wanted to prove just how tenuous it was. Why else would I try to stop two children from doing nothing? Naturally they refused to obey me. But more was at stake here and we all knew it – our futures. Lisa and Alex were seizing an opportunity themselves: They were taking a stand against me, the intruder. It is one of the few moments in their lives when they have been in agreement. And I, in my muddleheaded way, continued to insist, 'Get out,' when what I really meant was, 'Let me in.'[1]

This is at the heart of the step-parenting dilemma: are we included, and if so why do we feel so excluded? We feel excluded because we are emphasising the wrong elements in our stepfamily matrix. Because the tie between parent and child is so strong, it's all too easy for a newcomer to assume that this is the only yardstick for measuring family relationships. And of course, if we rely on this yardstick we are doomed to feel insecure. Because we are neither a parent nor a child we are left feeling like a nothing.

This can become an acute problem, as one now adult stepdaughter testified:

My stepmother has so little confidence . . . she thinks she's unimportant, even though she's been with my dad for more than ten years and they have a child. She's really possessive over my dad and isn't entirely straight . . . she's sly and doesn't want my dad to see me when she isn't around. So he never comes to see me without her. I can see exactly how her mind works because I'm quite a beady person. When I ring up my dad, I can hear her listening in on our conversation . . . she thinks I don't know that she's there listening, but I do. It's sad really. She's such a mess. I do love her – she isn't a bad person – but I feel sorry for her too.

The stepmother in the above case study could not tolerate her partner having an independent relationship with his own children; she had to be in on everything or else she could not cope. If only this woman had been strong enough to let her husband get on with his kids free of her surveillance.

Rivalries in stepfamilies have a damaging, almost seductive power. In order to let go of this competitive edge, we have to hatch a different approach. The nuts and bolts of our situation do not change but our attitude can. Successful step-parenting is above all else a state of mind.

Practical Exercise

Go back to your Step-parenting Record and use it as a private document to own up to some of those reactions of which you are less than proud. Getting this oppressive stuff out and on to the page for your eyes only will help to normalise much of what you are experiencing and should also take away the guilty sting of the green-eyed monster.

1. Open the record at a double-page spread. On the left-hand side write down every single instance which provoked wrath and/or jealousy. Go into as much detail as you like and be as angry as you like
2. Use the right-hand page to work out exactly what you wanted from this situation but did not get. Was it time alone with your partner? More attention? More appreciation from your stepchildren? Or were you jealous of a fantasy perfect life that you can never achieve?
3. Define those situations that tip you over the edge and resolve to protect yourself by relying on the first cornerstone: YOU AND YOUR PARTNER ARE A TEAM

Rewriting the Rules

At some time or other most step-parents have felt threatened by their stepchildren. Such 'rivalries are next to impossible to avoid', as acknowledged by the leading stepfamily psychologist team of Emily and John Visher.[2] So instead of beating yourself up about feeling rivalrous, you have to take action to contain these perfectly normal psychological tussles. The first stage in this process is recognising that you are in fact wrestling with two different strands of emotional envy, one engendered by our stepchildren, the other by our partner.

A step-parent tends to be intimidated by the unshakeable position of a natural child. The quality of love that binds a parent to his or her child can seem so much more solid than the fluid love of a sexual relationship. We are intolerant of the amount of love these youngsters not only require but deserve, and believe somehow that attention given to them means less attention for us. Meanwhile, as the mother or father of our stepchildren, our partner receives something that is off-limits to us: the absolute love of his or her offspring. We long to be in their shoes, secure in the total warmth of their blood tie. We look at our partners and see someone who is completely at ease with these youngsters, the last thing that many of us feel around our stepkids. The comparison leaves us feeling more than a little sore.

As step-parents we lack experience. We are under-confident and wish that we knew what we were doing. Both our stepchildren and our partner seem much more grounded and able to slot into this peculiar stepfamily set-up; their shared past stands them in good stead. Despite the new configuration, everyone else has the confidence to express themselves; to cry, to swear and shout and rage about. Step-parents, particularly the female variety, tend not to express themselves. We internalise the thoughts that we are ashamed of, keeping our jealousy to ourselves. Step-parenting is a solitary endeavour; each of us tries not to mind about the communion from which we are excluded.

To quote Delia Ephron once again, struggling to make peace with her life as a stepmother:

> When I cooked my own goose, Lisa wouldn't eat it. Because I can cook all I want, but I can't feed. Feeding is what mothers do, and here Lisa drew the line. 'I'm not hungry,' she said, or something equally upsetting, like, 'I just feel like eating yogurt tonight.' It was her way of saying, 'You can't mother me.' So, at least in part, my efforts were thwarted. I was getting little payoff for my hard work. Though I succeeded in becoming indispensable to Larry, I wasn't satisfied. I wanted love. Lisa's love. I wanted this even before I loved Lisa myself, for its symbolic meaning – that I belonged in the family. Oh, what an unreasonable expectation. The self-centeredness of it.[3]

This writer succeeded in turning a critical eye on her own behaviour. She could see where she was going wrong, in setting her sights on an unrealistic goal: she 'wasn't satisfied' with being indispensable to Larry. She craved more, something that she didn't have. Perpetually looking ahead, yearning for all that is out of reach, is one of the most exhausting aspects of human nature. It amounts to a permanent sense of dissatisfaction with our lot, that what we have is not enough and that we need more if we are to be happy. Stepfamilies are fundamentally different from intact families. It is hopeless to pretend otherwise. And yet this is a trap that many step-parents fall into simply because there are no alternatives out there. Now is the time to be explicit about what makes a stepfamily quite so different.

- You and your partner have set up home together. As a couple you are forging a shared existence which makes both of you happy
- Whether your stepchildren live with you full-time or part-time, your relationship with them is a secondary matter
- Your partnership is of ultimate importance, giving you *all*

the justification you need for your position in the stepfamily
- You do *not* need to justify your presence to your stepchildren in any way, e.g. by trying to earn their affection, approval or love. Emotionally you need *only the basic minimum of respect* from your stepchildren
- It is up to your partner to set about demonstrating that his or her children must afford you a basic degree of respect

Learning Control

Most step-parents have to learn to discipline their emotional responses. If we want to distinguish ourselves from our step-children, we must use the wisdom that supposedly comes with our years. Somebody has to be a grown-up in this situation and it's definitely us. What is required is a ruthlessly strict approach with the subject under scrutiny: you.

As soon as you become aware of the first tremor of jealousy, take yourself in hand. Ask yourself the following questions:

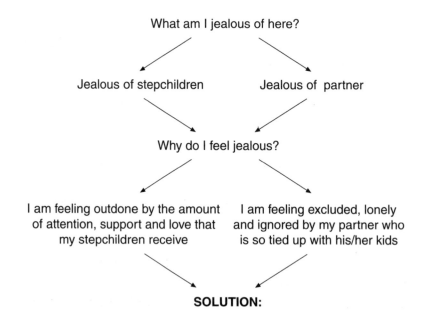

What am I jealous of here?

Jealous of stepchildren   Jealous of partner

Why do I feel jealous?

I am feeling outdone by the amount of attention, support and love that my stepchildren receive

I am feeling excluded, lonely and ignored by my partner who is so tied up with his/her kids

SOLUTION:

Remember that the roles of parent and lover are quite distinct. You have your partner as a lover and do not need him/her as a parent. But coping with the fact that the stepchildren have no love for their step-parent can be a great strain on you. To cope with the strain, *take solace in the strength of your partnership*. This is the only important thing.

Talk to your partner about all the difficulties that you are encountering. Make sure that as a team you work together to create a solid, productive and strong foundation for your stepfamily, for your partnership is at the heart of your stepfamily. It has enough power to combat insecurity.

Once you are feeling secure in your partnership, you can simultaneously:

- Give your partner the space and freedom to be a parent
- Release yourself from expecting affection/love from your stepchildren

In other words, you'll have the confidence to look for support from the right quarters and let the rest alone.

Correcting Your Emphasis

Realising that you have an ally is the key to transforming your relationship with your stepchildren. Allowing yourself to tap into the strength offered by your partner is the way out of the hellish love triangle that fractures many a stepfamily. You and your partner are not just a couple, you are a *team*.

This may not sound like the epitome of romance. However, when it comes to stepfamily life, teamwork is what counts. Because your partner and his or her children can be defined as being on the same biological team, you in turn need to feel supported by the team of your partnership. Clearly both these groupings overlap, but what's important is that everyone is included.

Realigning your focus back on to your partnership releases you from the painful dynamic of newcomer v. blood relatives. Your position is no longer isolated. Re-evaluate your partnership and learn to appreciate its inherent success. Take the warmth and strength that exists between the two of you and use it to help you deal with the stepchildren. The fact of the matter is that your partner loves you so much that he or she has chosen to share his or her life with you. The pair of you are building a future together, and the entity of your couple represents an enormous amount on both a private and a public level. In the eyes of the world, you are part of a unit, where your love for your partner is recognised and reciprocated. This bond between the two of you is one of the most significant elements in your life. Your partnership anchors your daily routine, grounding you, providing security and giving you direction. It is something to be celebrated, not taken for granted.

And yet as soon as children from a previous relationship are introduced, taking our partnership for granted is exactly what we start to do. At a time when it would be sensible to remember what binds us to the mother or father of these children, we concentrate solely on the reactions of the stepchildren to both ourselves and our partner. Although this is an easy mistake to make, it is a disastrous one.

Your partner no doubt is confident that he or she understands the difficulties of your position. This confidence however is misplaced. The only exception is if you too have children from a previous relationship. If both of you are step-parents, then and only then can you simultaneously understand the nature of the challenge. But this state of affairs is less common. Most restructured families include only one step-parent. Which is why you are on your own until your partner takes the trouble to bring you in from the cold.

That you are the uncertain newcomer requesting entry into a pre-existing family group is plain for all to see. As the person who introduced you into the group, your partner is well aware of the facts. And this is what their understanding is based on: the facts. The desire to have you there insulates your partner from the emotional reality of your experience as a step-parent. According to your partner, this is a straightforward business. There are the kids, playing over there; all you have to do is be normal and everything will be fine, right?

But frequently everything is not fine. The insistence of a partner that there isn't a problem here only makes things worse. Biological parents are programmed to think that their kids are absolutely, impossibly wonderful and worth defending at every turn. If a new girlfriend or boyfriend dares to hint that he or she is experiencing difficulty around the kids, this tests the boundaries big-time.

Your difficulties get wrongly processed by the parent, who ends up thinking that you are having a go at his or her kids. When you are simply expressing some of the problems that you're having, your partner only hears you criticising his or her kid.

The following conversation makes this point clearly:

Step-parent: When I picked Tim up from school today, he was furious . . .

Parent: Yeah, well, he finds it tiring, you know. And he doesn't like his teacher at all . . .

Step-parent: It was embarrassing really. He yelled at me, saying he hated it when I picked him up. He kept screaming, 'Where's my dad?' Everyone stared, even the teacher.

Parent: God, people are so nosy, aren't they? Enough to make you weep, isn't it?

Step-parent: Actually I did weep, not that Tim saw. Just a tear . . . it was so humiliating, like he hates my guts!

Parent: Come on, he's not a bad kid. He didn't mean it!
                 He must have had a really bad day. I wonder if I
                 should talk to his teacher, what do you think?

Without realising, the parent in the above example responds only as a parent. Anxiety about Tim's well-being totally eclipses the troubles of the step-parent, which are inadvertently sidelined and ultimately ignored. This is not a conscious process: it happens almost automatically, as a result of the biological programming. But it leaves the step-parent feeling lousy. At a time when this person was looking for reassurance, the cupboard was bare.

Just as we are making an enormous effort to come to terms with the new dynamic, our partners must make an effort of similar magnitude. If the two of you are to survive as a couple and if the lot of you are to survive as a stepfamily, your partner must broaden his or her focus.

It's difficult for anyone to accept that their new partner is struggling to get along with his or her kids. First, there's all the protective instinct of a bioparent already discussed. Second, there's a furious determination to make things work. Your partner loves you and loves the kids and does not want problems. And it's part of our psyche that when we don't want to see something, we often don't see it, even if it is right there in all its three-dimensional glory, with a furious step-parent in one corner, a furious stepchild in the other and a parent in the middle saying, 'Nobody's really cross, are they?' In other words, problems are often suppressed as a way of pretending that everything's fine.

Although a parent is inclined to pretend in this way, a step-parent is less inclined. We may go along with the pretence for a while, as we too are motivated to make a go of our stepfamily. But what we really want and need is support. And there is only one person that we need it from: our partner.

Learning Dialogue

Strong relationships are based on endorsement. When two people value each other, a friendship can flourish. An employer communicates approval by raising salaries. Lovers bill and coo a stream of sweet nothings. A hard-working nurse cares for a grateful patient. And yet much of step-parenting is a thankless task. Getting used to this reality is an ordeal which is the subject of the second cornerstone: KNOW YOUR ROLE. For our purposes here, it's sufficient to say that a step-parent is often shocked by just how little feedback he or she receives from the stepchildren. This in itself is something that a partner often fails to notice; what is adequate thanks for a parent is frequently inadequate thanks for a step-parent.

Children take their biological parents for granted, and that often seems fine to Mum or Dad. Being taken for granted does not however seem fine to a stepfather or stepmother. This is just one of many discrepancies in outlook that separates parent from step-parent. For the health of your partnership, it is essential that these differences are openly acknowledged, discussed and resolved.

It's perfectly normal for stepchildren to restrict the amount of feedback they give to a step-parent. Whether they do this consciously or unconsciously is open to debate but the net result is the same: a step-parent feels ignored. And being ignored is not good for anyone's self-esteem. To stop a step-parent's spirits from sinking, a partner must step in and shoulder responsibility. After all, this situation has been created by your partner. It's up to him or her to look after your well-being, just as you do your level best to look after their well-being, and that is what makes you a couple.

Although your partner obviously wants you to be happy, he or she instinctively bolsters the confidence of the person they know: the lover. You are reassured as that person, soothed by your shared intimacy and merged lives. But when you are wearing your step-parenting hat, you need a very different kind of reassurance, and this is what catches many a partner off-guard.

Unless you too have children from a previous relationship, you are now honouring a duty which your partner does not have to honour. The fact that you are taking on an additional burden needs to be recognised by your partner. Unless that recognition is forthcoming, a step-parent is left floundering, resentful and alone.

When it comes to stepfamily life, both partners need some education. It's a steep learning curve for the step-parent, no doubt about that. But your partner must also learn to support you not only as a lover but as a stepmother or father. What this means is being able to talk frankly about the entire range of difficulties that a step-parent is encountering, without assuming the kids are under attack. You have to carve out some neutral territory which is reserved for parent-to-step-parent discussion.

The Mechanics of Dialogue

Being able to listen and respond constructively is an important skill in any family. It is however particularly important in a stepfamily, where all of you have to make an effort to communicate as you learn the ropes of living together (see page 38). On the private level of your partnership, listening to each other is imperative if the differing outlooks of parent and step-parent are to be reconciled. The following case history clearly illustrates the damaging consequences of non-communication:

When Eleanor married Robert, she had no problem with his four-year-old son. Andrew lived with his mother but would come for contact visits. Due to concerns about Andy's welfare, the mother lost custody of her son, who now came to live with his father, Eleanor and their six-month-old baby.

This was when the problems started. Robert devoted his energies to settling Andy into his new home. Eleanor felt rejected, for herself and for their child. She felt angry and blamed herself because she did not love Andy. Her feelings of exclusion were compounded by Robert's insistence that he alone should determine Andy's domestic arrangements. She resented the fact that she had to care for a child whom she was not allowed to control.

Andy's behaviour deteriorated, Robert did not discipline his son and Eleanor became depressed. She sought the help of a therapist. In therapy, Eleanor came to realise that at no stage had she actually told Robert what she needed in order to be happy. The perceived injustice of her position had been suppressed, making her feel alienated from the 'family' of Robert and Andy. Slowly she learned how to verbalise her own needs, which included tackling the thorny issue of who should discipline Andy. Robert came to realise that Eleanor had to discipline Andy as she was the principal homemaker. Instead of working separately they began to work together.[4]

As this example makes clear, fault can lie on both sides of the parent/step-parent divide. It was only with hindsight that Eleanor realised that she was blocking out her frustrations. Because she told Robert nothing, he did not appreciate the strain she was under. Nor did he appreciate that if a step-parent is to provide care then they must be empowered with some authority. Simultaneously charging someone to look after a child whilst depriving them of responsibility is a contradiction in terms.

Sometimes it takes a therapist to get a couple talking about the conflicts they encounter in stepfamily life. But when the spirit is willing on both sides, it's more than possible for a couple to learn this skill on their own terms and in their own time. You want your stepfamily to cohere as a single unit but you can only forge unity through talking, and then talking some more, and rounding off with a grand finale of . . . you guessed it, a proper talk.

Step-parent and parent need to collaborate because:

- A step-parent is under pressure: coping with the imbalance of giving a great deal to but receiving little from the stepchildren is stressful

- If we receive no endorsement from our stepchildren, we need to make sure that we are getting sufficient endorsement from somewhere else: our partner must step into the breach
- It is the parent's responsibility to provide a listening ear and reassurance

Remember the rules of dialogue:

- A parent must exercise self-discipline and learn to hear out what the step-parent has to say without jumping to the conclusion that his or her child is being criticised
- You and your partner have to go into training to get this dialogue up and running. Don't be afraid to be painfully honest
- Every step-parent requires respect for the hard work they put in and it's your partner's duty to directly provide that respect and also to instil it in his/her children
- It is up to your partner to demonstrate that the two of you are absolutely indivisible. All stepchildren find it difficult to digest the fact that their parent has formed an unbreakable alliance with a new adult. Although you can stand up for yourself, your stepchildren need to hear the awful truth – that the two of you are a team – from their parent

Constructive dialogue has its own momentum. The pair of you will know when you are getting somewhere and it'll be an exhilarating feeling. Being at the helm of a stepfamily puts your partnership to the test in ways that are unimaginable to an intact family. If you rise to the challenge, you can share a massive pride in your joint achievement.

Practical Exercise

Here the task is to devise a crystal-clear phrase that summarises your teamwork. Use this phrase to shore up your confidence when you are feeling at a low ebb. This is the purpose of affirmations: they create an internal support system to keep you out of danger. Devise your own personal affirmation by:

1. Taking your partner's strongest assertion of his or her faith in you
2. Using these words as an effective weapon against isolation/jealousy, e.g. 'The only thing I need is Joe's love. He thinks I'm amazing. I can handle this because I've got him'
3. Imagine or recall a situation which might provoke jealousy. Repeat your affirmation. Does it calm you down? If not, come up with something even more powerful. Now do you feel pepped up when you repeat the magic words?

Respect and Courtesy

Now that your partner is alive to the stresses of step-parenting and you are buoyed up as a result, both of you have come to appreciate the importance of the united front. And part of functioning as a team is being seen to function as a team.

Even within the enclosed setting of your home, your partnership operates on two levels. There is private dialogue in which the two of you thrash out your common ground, and then there's also the front that both of you present to the others, to your stepchildren, to an ex-spouse, to grandparents – all of whom have to learn to live with the fact that the two of you are a team.

Standing up for a beleaguered step-parent is an essential technique for anyone who wants to bring about stepfamily integration.

Children in particular are keen to distance their parent from this new partner. The easiest way of doing this is by complaining, loudly and endlessly, about whatever it is that a step-parent happens to be doing or saying. And this is when their mum or dad has to blow the whistle and wave the red card. Defending your partner is written into every strong union. The two of you are only going to be taken seriously as a team if you behave like a team, not just sometimes, but all the time.

Once your partner starts publicly defending you in front of your stepchildren, you can enjoy an increased sense of security. You will no longer feel excluded or jealous but relax into the role, secure in the knowledge that your partner appreciates you deeply both as a lover and as a step-parent.

Respect is of course something that the two of you already have for each other. However, the process of instilling respect in reluctant stepchildren is a different matter. Nevertheless, this process is unavoidable if you are to make a success of your step-family. If a stepchild is flagrantly rude, he or she must be taken aside by their bioparent, who carefully explains that such behaviour is unacceptable.

And then for the hard part: the stepchild must apologise. A parent is under an obligation to secure this apology. It may take a little while, hours rather than minutes, or possibly even days. But that apology has to come if your teamwork is to be taken seriously. Turn back to the fictional conversation between a non-communicating parent and step-parent on page 55. In this scenario, a stepmother has been humiliated and upset by the rejecting behaviour of stepson Timmy. If there are no repercussions for this kind of open aggression, Timmy will carry on believing that he can treat his stepmother in this way. Alternatively, if his father takes him to one side and explains that it is not kind to be so hurtful, the child will be forced to rethink his approach.

Obviously, sticking up for each other only affects how your

stepfamily gets along on the surface. Insisting on the occasional 'sorry' cannot change the way a stepchild feels, but it should influence how they behave. And this is half the battle. This can be a complicated issue for the pivotal parent/partner figure, who may find it hard standing up for a partner when this simultaneously turns into a reprimand. It all comes down to loyalty. A parent will always be loyal to their child. But they also have to learn to be loyal to their partner in front of their kids, even when this feels like a hard course to follow.

Practical Exercise

Take the time to go through the agenda below with your partner, making sure that you both air your feelings on each issue. Discuss the extent to which you agree on these objectives and if you disagree, find a point on which you can compromise.

The step-parent undertakes to:

1. Accept the stepchildren as a vital, permanent part of life, and not to resent their presence
2. Allow the parent full access to his/her children without being jealous
3. Talk to her/his partner about any difficulty they are experiencing
4. Believe that she/he is a valued person within the new unit of the stepfamily. Over time their stepchildren will appreciate their contribution

The parent undertakes to:

1. Include the step-parent within the close-knit 'blood' family group
2. Be aware that his/her partner may be feeling excluded/jealous
3. Listen, provide support and reassure the struggling step-parent
4. Remember that he/she can give their partner all they need by reaffirming the strength of the partnership

5. Realise that although they and their partner are equals, they are not both equal in the eyes of the stepchildren: they want their parent more

5. Realise that this inequality can be problematic: it is easy for the step-parent to feel rejected in the circumstances

6. Accept that they must not criticise or interfere unduly in the way their partner parents the stepchildren

6. Be aware that the step-parent can feel frustrated/impotent precisely because they are not the parent

7. Learn to let their partner be their main defender; the stepchildren need to see that the pair of you work as one team

7. Put forward the step-parent's case to critical/hostile stepchildren

8. Be realistic about their partner's contact with their ex: it is unavoidable and they must step back and be tolerant

8. Be aware that contact with their ex can be very hard for their partner

9. Take the long-term view: time will resolve much conflict

9. Be patient with the struggling step-parent. Integration does not happen overnight

Communication Inhibitors

Acknowledging the different pressures that both step-parent and parent are under is absolutely crucial if both of you are to create a shared value system. Of course it can be tricky getting to the heart of the matter. There are genuine obstacles that prevent honest one-to-one exchange. Awareness of what can get in the way will help you track past these obstacles and clear some of the dead wood that stops progress.

1. *Guilt on the part of the step-parent.* Many step-parents try to squeeze themselves into the shoes of the absent biological parent. We do this because we think we should, and because society does not present us with any alternatives specifically tailored to our role. But the net result of trying to be a mother or a father to our stepchildren is that it leaves us feeling guilty.

We all know that a biological parent feels unconditional love for his or her offspring; unfortunately we do not begin our lives as step-parent with this blessing in the bag. So what happens when jealousy gets the better of us? How are we meant to feel when anger makes us scream the house down? What happens when we look at our stepchildren without affection? We feel guilty about these ugly emotions.

This guilt about our lack of enthusiasm for or downright resentment of our stepchildren becomes a dark secret which we cannot share with our partner. This sense of shame is perhaps the most significant barrier to communication. At times our reactions make us feel so awkward that owning up to them seems impossible.

Be brave and remind yourself that this ambivalence is entirely normal. Nobody ever said you had to feel like your stepchild's mother or father. Your role, which is underpinned by the second cornerstone, is not to be a parent but to be a supplementary figure in the lives of your stepchildren. So put aside this unhelpful standard and learn to admit what you are experiencing. Your partner can only be supportive if you let him or her know exactly what is going wrong.

2. *Guilt on the part of the parent.* Children in stepfamilies have by definition suffered the loss of living full-time with both their natural parents. Whether through relationship breakdown or bereavement, separations of this kind leave a legacy of regret, sadness and yearning for something that cannot be. Watching

your child go through this ordeal is traumatic for everyone. Many parents never shake off their guilt.

Unless you too have been through a similar break-up, it can be hard for a new partner to appreciate the oppressive nature of this burden. Personally, it took me a long time to realise the extent of my husband's guilt about getting divorced. When his daughters came to stay, he worried over them obsessively, desperate not to cause them any more pain. He was their best daddy and he was going to do all he could to keep their universe calm from now on. If that meant closing ranks against the alien stepmother, then so be it. This was needless to say pretty hard to bear.

But we sweated through by thrashing out these painful issues. Acquiring the habit of constructive dialogue is just like acquiring any new skill: it takes practice, determination and time.

3. *Pride*. Frequently guilt about our performance is overlaid with a damaging layer of pride. None of us likes admitting that we are being defeated by a situation. None of us wants to feel like a failure. And yet sometimes we have to hit rock bottom if things are to improve. Have the courage to be honest. The temporary loss of face is worth it in the long run.

Everyone Benefits from Team Loyalty

The Step-parent

Being a step-parent means being two different people at once. First off, you are one half of a strong couple, someone who is valued and respected by their lover. Yet your presence can be entirely overlooked by this same individual when his or her children are around. One minute the two of you could not be closer, the next you are being treated like a virtual stranger.

This ebb and flow of loyalties is typical of many stepfamilies. The sense of your partner slipping away from you is disorientating; it brings out the worst in you, making you angry, jealous or just plain depressed. The ongoing cycle of inclusion and exclusion is severely taxing, amplifying existing tensions within the step-family. The parent must make every effort to combine forces with step-parent or else chaos will ensue as the following case history clearly demonstrates.

When Elizabeth Jane Howard married Kingsley Amis in 1970, she became stepmother to his children, Martin and Philip. The boys chose to live with their father and his new wife. They were aged fifteen and thirteen at the time, immersed in adolescent angst and rebellion and utterly hostile to their stepmother, whom they believed had caused the break-up of their parents' marriage. With hindsight, Elizabeth Howard now attributes the difficulties she had as a stepmother to the absence of any working partnership between her and her husband.

> It was in fact my suggestion that the boys come to live with us because their mother wasn't coping at all well. But I really had no idea what I was letting myself in for. Things would have been much easier if Kingsley had concerned himself with the practical side of life, but as it was all left to me – meals, routine, discipline.
>
> On the occasions when I needed backing up, Kingsley failed to support me at all, tending to side with the boys against me. Looking back on it, the lack of understanding between us was the root of the problem. I tried to talk to him about the boys, but even though he was their father, he simply wasn't interested.

The discord inherent in this situation stemmed from a failure to combine the needs of the adult generation into one coherent front. Fusing the different outlooks of parent and step-parent into a single, unified approach will bring the cycle of inclusion and exclusion to an end. A new climate of continuity replaces the awkward perception that your partner is only sometimes there for you.

Once the pair of you have cemented the emotional foundations of your alliance it becomes possible to trust in your partner safeguarding your interests at all times. Instead of having an occasional ally, you have a permanent ally. The step-parent gains increasing confidence as his or her input is endorsed and defended by the step-parent.

As a couple, we learned this lesson the hard way. One of our worst rows ever had its roots in our failure to work together. One midweek night when my husband was due back late, I put his daughters to bed. Except they wouldn't go to bed – they went bonkers instead. High-jinks, hysterical laughter, bedtime antics of every shape and size. I was cooking supper for a friend but I kept going up to their bedroom and telling them to calm down. Then there were the warnings, and finally I lost my temper at which point they did quieten down. Soon after, Daddy came home and went up to see his girls first thing. Minutes later he walked into the kitchen ashen-faced. 'How dare you treat my girls like that?' He was spitting with anger.

I felt shocked. My friend was embarrassed. As far as I was concerned, it had been a perfectly normal situation of bedtime frolics which had to be brought to an end. But my stepdaughters had painted a different picture. Furious with me, Daddy stormed downstairs demanding an explanation before I could say a word. The injustice of it all wound me up – and how.

The repercussions of that argument went on for quite a while. It left me numb and empty. We were poles apart in our attitudes to that situation, which in turn signalled a more fundamental polarity which kept us at opposite ends of our stepfamily. A rethink was essential if we were to survive.

Meltdowns of this kind can however be productive. Research relating specifically to stepmothers[5] describes three distinct stages of assimilation into the stepfamily:

1. Initial feelings towards stepchildren are usually positive. If the stepmother does not take to them immediately, there is

usually the strong presence of denial. During this 'honeymoon period' everyone tries to be on best behaviour

2. Soon the stepmother begins to notice some negative feeling she has towards her stepchildren. Yet she hides her feelings as she does not want to go through a painful divorce or experience failure

3. Eventually there is some kind of crisis. The stepmother must share her worries with her partner, and then this creates an opportunity to solve conflict

Some couples manage to forge joint principles without the trigger of a crisis. The rest of us close our eyes to what we do not want to see until a situation blows up that forces us to address the difficult issues we have been repressing.

The circumstances that prompt this discussion are unimportant; all that matters is that the discussion takes place and that you as the step-parent come to believe that your partner is always going to look after your interests. In return, you are promising to do your absolute best not only by furthering your relationship with your stepchildren but also by allowing your partner the freedom to enjoy his or her children without restriction. This is the basis of your contract. From now on you have a blueprint for stepfamily stability.

The Parent

Parents also benefit from team loyalty. Anyone who is the linchpin figure in the love triangle is under considerable pressure and frequently feels torn between the conflicting demands of partner and children. Balance can only be achieved between the two factions once the two adults have consolidated their identity as one unbreakable axis.

A parent is automatically allied to his or her children. This alliance increases in intensity following the upset of relationship breakdown or bereavement: the urge to protect kicks in as a mother or father tries to ward off further pain. Many parents simply do not realise that they are working to preserve the status quo of their original family unit.

Consequently, the incoming step-parent is sidelined; he or she pulls in one direction, and the children in another. But if a parent can endorse his or her partnership as the foundation of the new stepfamily, instead of being pulled in two different directions, he or she is able to commit to a single purpose of bringing about a better future.

The Stepchildren

Few children willingly embrace their mum or dad's new partner. On the surface they may (or may not) go through the motions of civility, but accepting a parent's new partner is a huge and diffi-cult adjustment. Unless their parent makes a point of demonstrating that the pair of you are a permanent item, the children will resist making that adjustment.

Most children cling to the belief that their mum and dad belong to each other. The flipside of this belief is often a secret fantasy that their parents will one day be reunited. I became acutely aware of this when one of my stepdaughters asked her father one day why he didn't live with them any more. He gave the usual answer about not getting along with her mummy. 'But you and Mummy don't fight now, so you should come back, shouldn't you?' There was not a lot he could say. I had been on the scene for a few years, and we already had two children, but all this was quite irrelevant as far as this little girl was concerned.

Children fuel their dreams by trying to oust the step-parent. Whether they do this consciously or unconsciously varies from one child to the next, but their hidden agenda remains the same. They want to perceive their mother or father as quite separate from the irksome new partner and test out the waters by pitching parent against step-parent.

This was pretty much what happened in that argument we had all those years ago: my stepdaughters wanted to see whose side their dad was going to take, mine or theirs.

It doesn't do children any favours to let them believe that they can manipulate their parents' lives. It is much better for all concerned if the parent has the strength to make a show of absolute commitment to the new partnership. It's only in this way that a stepchild can begin to accept an outsider. They have to see that their mother or father will protect you to the hilt. Why? Because you are the person who makes him or her happy. Over time most stepchildren come to respect a step-parent for this reason. I interviewed one adult who had never had a strong rapport with his stepmother but had this to say in her favour:

It wasn't that we got along badly, but we didn't get along that well either. She was so nervous with us, like a rabbit caught in the headlights.

I was just gone twenty when we first met, so I had my own life down in London and they were up in Yorkshire. Because she kept her distance, I kept mine and we just had nothing in common for years and years.

But recently there was something about the two of them that really struck me: they were just so happy together. And even though she never lets on anything to me, she obviously makes my dad happy. And I'm grateful for that, and that's really why I can accept her now, because she makes him happy.

In presenting a united front, you are not asking the stepchildren to abandon their private dreams about reunion. All you are doing is helping them to adjust. If this strategy is consistently followed, the younger generation will slowly stop fighting against the solidity of your partnership and settle into the rhythm of life as it is now.

Providing a Positive Model

The psychologist Jerry Lewis found that if the relationship between the spouses is strong and can withstand attempts by the children to split or weaken the alliance, the family unit is able to cope successfully.[6]

As a couple, in pledging to be mutually loyal, supportive and understanding you are not only consolidating your relationship but also demonstrating to your stepchildren that the two of you get along just fine and they can do the same.

Adjusting to stepfamily life is hard for everyone. By getting along with each other, a couple is creating an atmosphere which encourages stepchildren to let go of old prejudices. The pair of you have to lead by example and show everyone concerned that it's OK to kick back and be one big happy stepfamily.

These adjustments that you're making are substantial. To make shifts of this magnitude requires a lot of energy, more energy in fact than can be reasonably expected of one person. That is why you must look to your partner for all the help, guidance and strength that you will need along the way. Your partner is after all the reason that you're a step-parent in the first place. He or she is under an obligation to support you through this mammoth undertaking.

As step-parents to angry children we have to learn to override our instinct to back away from those who spurn us. The energy for this effort of will must spring from the core of our partnership: if we feel loved we can be loving towards even hostile stepchildren. Good step-parenting is a joint responsibility.

5

Teamwork in Practice

Getting to grips with the theory is one thing, translating it into practice is quite another. How the pair of you handle the business of running your stepfamily is the acid test of your teamwork.

Families are defined by their own particular routines and traditions. An incoming step-parent can feel quite paralysed by the unfamiliarity of this new environment. They know little about this particular band of kith and kin or the pattern of their communal lives. So what is the incoming step-parent meant to do – slot into the existing structure and pretend that they've been there all along? In other words, what happens to a family when a step-parent moves in?

Like it or not, the arrival of a step-parent marks the end of the pre-existing family group and the birth of something new: a stepfamily. But this truth can be a source of fear to your step-children and possibly for your partner too. Gaining a step-parent means saying goodbye to their past as a single biological unit. Because this can spell loss, the whole concept of starting over has to be handled with great sensitivity by both you and your partner.

According to Visher and Visher, 'The fact that patterns solidified over a number of years have suddenly become questioned may lead to daily conflict, contributing to the degree of anxiety experienced by the couple as well as by the children in the step-family'.[1] Gaining a step-parent means gaining some of their way of doing things, which can seem pretty alien, as this stepson made clear:

> I'd been living in Morocco with my mum and when I came back to England aged nine, I went to live with my dad and his new wife. It was the first time I'd met my stepmother. She asked me to fetch the milk from the fridge, and their milk was still delivered, in those glass bottles, you know.
>
> And in front of everyone, I shook it up and down, shaking vigorously because I remembered my British grandmother telling me that was the right thing to do. And my stepmother shrieked, 'No, no, no! What on earth are you doing?' She was all in a fluster, and it was all because she loved the cream on the top of the milk, and now thanks to me, there was no cream. It was like, Ah! So there's one lot of rules in my granny's house and here the rules are completely different. It was quite an eye opener . . .

This account illustrates the strain imposed on children who are members of two households. Everyone benefits from knowing what's expected of them, but an incoming step-parent must be flexible and not dogmatic. In formulating some of the basics that are part of every family's routine, we have to exercise care. 'The couple in the stepfamily have more chance of success and a reduction of tension if they are sensitive to the fact that the children will need time to assume a suitable role in the family and cannot be forced into one,'[2] say Visher and Visher.

Finding the Right Rhythm for Your Household

Domestic life is largely a matter of limits; what is and is not allowed to take place in your home defines the character of your household. Choosing what to prioritise, what to relegate to the second division and what to outlaw can be a difficult business. And yet we all realise the significance of this type of domestic legislation. By making clear what is tolerated and what is not, a family is not only looking after but also educating the next generation.

Arguably stepfamilies have a greater need for boundaries than their intact counterparts. Divisions have to be bridged and a sense of unity created. Clear messages about the daily routine, acceptable behaviour and nascent traditions help all concerned to work out how they slot into the new matrix, though step-parents are often afraid of being disliked if they insist that house rules be obeyed. But even the most timid step-parent has to have the courage to put these fears to one side and get on with the job. All the emotional issues should be kept separate from the business of running a household. In being clear about what is expected of everyone in a day-to-day way, you are removing a burden of doubt.

In order to provide that certainty, you and your partner need to agree on how to manage the universals set out below. Remember this is about regulating a home, not dishing out discipline. Homes should be places of refuge.

Children react against limits whether they are in step- or intact families. Arguably the struggle is greater when a step-parent is involved as his or her claim to authority is not necessarily recognised. One way of getting round this problem is to actively involve the stepchildren. If they are old enough to take part in sensible talk, then the family council is a really useful way of bringing everyone together.

The Stepfamily Council

A regular slot that enables all of you to get stuff off your chest gives your stepfamily an enormous advantage. As the leading psychologists in this field state, 'If children are included, it will make them feel less like things are going on behind their backs. They will usually behave responsibly as a result.'[3]

If you can communicate effectively as a group, you are well on your way to pulling together as a stepfamily. So before you rule out the concept, consider some of the benefits of a stepfamily council:

1. It provides an inclusive environment in which everyone can participate. This can be particularly important for non-resident stepchildren, who have a tendency to believe that their vote doesn't count

2. A feeling of democracy is in the air. Even if this is an illusion, a meeting breaks down the hierarchical power structure of adults v. children. In the context of the meeting, you're all equal

3. Ultimately learning to work together as a single unit means that you have to communicate about the details. Councils are simply a way of speeding up the process. Give it a try. You'll be surprised

Here are some suggestions for organising the council.

- Forget formality. You can make your council as informal as you like by choosing a relaxed venue – outdoors or over a meal
- If you and your partner are nervous then call the first meeting on your own terms. Initially, this may mean not revealing the overall plan to your stepchildren, who might not like the idea. Launch a group discussion in the most casual way, like on a car journey, without institutionalising the process
- Keep the objective of the stepfamily council clearly in

mind: you are providing an opportunity where you can talk frankly to each other

- Anything can be up for discussion, good and bad: future plans, particular grievances, making an opinion heard or clarifying a house rule, having a laugh or saying sorry
- As the adults, you and your partner should not get frazzled by whatever the stepchildren have to say. What matters is that they feel they can get their complaints out into the open. Honesty is only possible if they do not feel intimidated by over-emotional grown-ups
- Some families have a suggestions box for posting subjects that need an airing. The box is always there and suggestions are read out at the meetings. Others have an agenda stuck up on the fridge. Going freestyle is fine too

During the first phase of stepfamily adjustment, it may be in everyone's interests if it is the parent and not the step-parent who presents the results of your discussions. In those very early days, a child can be reluctant to accept that Mum or Dad's new partner has any authority. As long as things remain delicate, the fiction that a step-parent has little or no input into a stepchild's welfare is allowed to continue. But as everyone gets used to each other, a step-parent grows more vocal.

Family life is an endless mosaic of small details. It's worth making the effort to consider these details, no matter how trivial they may seem. One stepmother told me that she used to hate mealtimes with her stepchildren. This was mainly because of an awkward rectangular kitchen table. Invariably her stepchildren would cluster round their dad at one end, leaving her isolated and lonely at the other. As soon as she diagnosed the source of the problem, she suggested to her husband that they buy a circular table so that nobody should feel left out. Initially reluctant, he thought she was making a mountain out of molehill. But this was a crucial matter that went right to the heart of how this woman felt about her stepfamily. After a little persistence a round table replaced the old model and from then on mealtimes became less of an ordeal. Getting these practical nuts and bolts into an order that works for everyone is an essential part of learning to live life as one stepfamily.

Whether or not your stepchildren are involved in the decision-making process, the following areas demand agreement of the two people at the helm of your stepfamily:

Mealtimes

Mealtimes crop up with alarming frequency. Sitting down to eat together is the backbone of family life. In an ideal world, sharing breakfast, lunch or supper should be a relaxed affair, catching up, having a laugh, enjoying each other's company. As such, meal-times feed body and soul.

For me personally, enjoying eating together was enormously important. This only becomes possible when everyone knows what to expect of each other and it can take a long time, especially if you're a non-custodial step-parent, to establish a template that works.

The absence of any other distractions can make the mealtime experience an alarming one. When unresolved issues still domi-nate, it's easy for these to be fraught times which are an endurance test for all concerned. This was certainly the case for the following stepmother, who told me:

> My stepdaughter is at a bad age and will not eat anything. She lives with her mum but when she's with us she's so picky it's untrue. My other half panders to her. This summer we were all on holiday, and Molly wouldn't touch the meal that we were all sit-ting down to eat. So David nipped off to make her some fishfingers. I mean, this drives me absolutely round the bend.

And of course my son, who's only six, would then say, 'I want fishfingers too!'

But I want him to eat with us, to learn to eat with the grown-ups. I said, 'I'm sorry, but you can't,' and then my son wails, 'But it's not fair! I want what Molly's got! Why is she allowed to and I'm not?' What can I say? I feel like screaming, 'She's got a different mother!' but I can't . . .

Precisely because everyone is gathered together, mealtimes are also a perfect opportunity for temper tantrums, which achieve maximum impact because everyone is watching. We had many years of off-the-wall behaviour at breakfasts, lunches and suppers.

But giving up on the idea of eating together is like giving up on your stepfamily itself. What needs to be focused on is how to make the experience less stressful.

The following aspects should be considered:

- Decide how often you are going to eat together and stick to this as a routine
- Resolve who is going to do the cooking and, if you've got a table full of fussy eaters, try to cook something that you know they like
- Make sure that you both agree on strategies to deal with a stepchild refusing to eat; a stepchild demanding to be given something different to eat; bad behaviour at table; a child who storms off and will not join the rest of you
- Try to find a middle path: neither you nor your partner should be so heavy-handed that mealtimes become torture but on the other hand the pair of you should be adult enough to enforce a few simple rules
- Make it clear what you expect of them in terms of table manners. This is a frequent bugbear of stepmothers in particular. Many fathers turn a blind eye, leaving their partner to pick up the pieces. Finding the middle ground

on this issue is vital as you don't want to turn into an etiquette dragon

- Looking after each other at mealtimes, e.g. passing the ketchup, is good practice for looking after each other in general terms
- Tell the children what they should do in terms of help: setting the table beforehand, taking their plates to the sink afterwards
- Have the confidence to stick to your rules. There's nothing mean or underhand about asking someone to follow house policy
- Remember that mealtimes should be fun. If the conversation isn't going very well, change tack. Quizzes are a good way of helping even the most sulky stepchild come out of his/her shell: competitions, guessing games, jokes, anything to break the ice
- Try not to bring up any issues that might provoke your stepchildren, e.g. their absent parent. Stick to safe topics to which everyone can contribute
- At the end of the meal, encourage the kids to thank the chef. This is particularly important when the step-parent has done the cooking!

Housekeeping

Homes do not run themselves. When a climate is created in which everyone contributes, even if this is only a token amount, a step-parent's tendency to feel taken for granted is kept to a minimum. Teenagers blasting the house down with loud music, untidy bedrooms and structuring leisure time all come under the umbrella of household rules.

Take a little time out together to establish what is and is not allowed under your roof. At the same time, think about what you want from the stepchildren in terms of a contribution. In the case of non-resident stepchildren this can be a delicate issue, as no stepchild wants to be put to work during a visit. But it's still worth fixing a couple of minor details and asking them to make this limited contribution.

What's significant here is not the actual task but going through the motions of helping. In families and stepfamilies alike, both adults and children are under an obligation to help out. My stepdaughters are obliged to do their bit even though they are only with us at weekends. They get all the benefits of being together and a little input confirms their place within the stepfamily.

As a step-parent, you do not want to be tiptoeing around your stepchildren. You need to have the confidence to be able to ask them to do basic chores. This is what happens in families of origin and stepfamilies should be no different in this respect.

In asking your stepchildren to pick up their toys or whatever, you are just behaving like any other responsible adult. The normality of your request can help to normalise the whole situation. Children behave better when they are forced to do so.

In short, it's well worth sorting out a little of who should be doing what, how and when. The resulting formula that sums up your household function creates a framework which consolidates your identity as a family. Some things to think about are:

- Jointly decide on the contribution you expect the stepchildren to make towards keeping house, e.g. helping set the table, putting their own dirty washing in the laundry basket, etc.
- Agree on what constitutes your private space and private property and make sure that this is communicated to and respected by the stepchildren
- Bear in mind that the parent's views on domestic issues are not more important; in this arena the step-parent must be allowed an equal say

- A step-parent is equally allowed to ask his/her stepchildren to follow the household rules. Do not fall into the trap of thinking that you can't ask them to tidy up. What a stepchild feels about you is not going to be affected by these mundane requests

- Have the confidence to tell them what you require of them. If you don't tell them what you want but suppress it all instead, you'll only end up resenting them and wishing that they were not in your space

- Endlessly repeating commands creates a tetchy atmosphere. Don't turn into a nag. Be patient about establishing routine – it will happen over time, not overnight

- Remember to acknowledge any positive contribution that your stepchildren make, no matter how small. Stepchildren flourish given a little praise. As often as possible tell them that they are doing well

- Be as relaxed as possible about general tidiness as this has a determining effect on the atmosphere within your home. If you place too great an emphasis on putting stuff away as soon as it gets pulled out of the cupboard, your stepchildren will feel that this space does not truly belong to them. Remember that this is their home too and an overflow of their possessions is natural enough. Sometimes when step-parent tension levels are rising, it's also worth standing back from the situation and asking yourself if what they are doing – jumping on your bed, playing games on your mobile phone – is really so unreasonable, or is it simply how any child would behave?

- Do not expect too much. Try not to invent new standards which the stepchildren fail to meet, e.g. Why didn't they help me with the packing (when in fact you hadn't asked them)?

- Be objective: if you feel that your stepchildren are not pulling their weight, ask yourself what is going on under the surface: do you feel taken for granted? undervalued? or simply unloved?
- Take time out: when the choice is between shouting at your stepchildren or leaving the room, you know which is the best option. Just learn to gauge when your pressure valve is about to blow and remove yourself from whatever is winding you up before it does blow
- Once the storm has passed, discuss the episode with your partner. Analyse what pushed you over the edge and make sure that you get the reassurance you need after the event. Better late than never!

Childcare

Voluntarily shouldering responsibility and then resenting what we have taken on is a speciality of step-parents. We want to make it work and so we embrace tasks as a way of demonstrating our commitment. The downside is that often we are quick to feel oppressed by the tasks that we have taken on.

Stepmothers in particular show initial enthusiasm when it comes to looking after their partner's children. The idea of playing Mummy or Daddy appeals, but the necessary emotional equipment is lacking. What needs to be assessed by the pair of you is:

- How much childcare can the step-parent realistically take on? Honesty is key here: it is perfectly fine to admit that you feel out of your depth or simply inexperienced. Be explicit about the difficulties you may be having, as your partner cannot read your mind
- Whether or not the step-parent is prepared to be in sole charge of the stepchildren. It's easy for a parent to assume that anyone can look after kids on their own, but for those

step-parents who have not had their own children, being left alone with the stepkids can be an alarming business. The limits of a step-parent's confidence in this area should be observed by the parent. Some specifics may be particularly troublesome, e.g. bathtime or bedtime, and these too should be acknowledged

- In blended families, which combine children from your partner's previous relationship with children from your present relationship, the distinction between the two batches of offspring is less sharp in your partner's eyes as he or she is parent to all of them. But as a step-parent the distinction remains valid. Nor should your partner forget that it is harder looking after children that are not biologically yours

- It's perfectly acceptable to say that you'd like a break. There is no rule that condemns you to twenty-four/seven childcare unless this is something that you are happy to provide. Mothers and fathers don't get a break but step-parents do!

Discipline

Step-parents are caught between a rock and a hard place when it comes to enforcing standards. Although you and your partner are working together to create a solid stepfamily, most step-children are wary of the idea that their step-parent has any authority over them at all. This is particularly true when step-families are still getting used to each other. One stepfather I interviewed summed this up neatly:

> I was always nervous of the idea of disciplining my stepchildren and one day I found out why. It was a disagreement at first, but then my stepson ended up pushing all my buttons. It happened so quickly, losing my temper. But there I was, about as angry as I

think I have ever been in my whole life. This poor kid was terrified. What he'd actually done was trivial compared with what he got.

All this stuff came out, I was so very angry, frightening really. My reaction was totally disproportionate, way too extreme. It was like I'd been waiting for this chance to rebel against these kids not loving me. That's what hurt. They were both so close to their mum, and I adored her too, and it was amazingly painful for the first two or three years. Still, I learned from my mistakes. Now I leave most of the discipline business to Lizzie.

This refusal to acknowledge a step-parent's influence is deeply frustrating when you and your partner are trying to keep the show on the road. Remarks along the lines of 'Don't tell me what to do! You're not my mum! You're not my dad!' can erode anyone's ability to cope. As a step-parent, your need to exercise control seems perfectly legitimate and yet you do not want to alienate mistrustful stepchildren.

A child instinctively accepts the principle of being disciplined by a mother or father, but this does not extend to the step-parent. However, once a bedrock of trust has been established, this positive can balance out the negative impact of any punitive action. In other words, as you prove yourself to be a permanent asset in their life, regulating your stepchildren becomes possible.

Demonstrating that you are a permanent part of the scenery happens much more quickly for full-time step-parents. When your stepchildren are resident, you will need to be an enforcer right from the start. You have a voice; just be careful how you use it. When it comes to helping your stepchildren do the right thing, the pair of you should be working as a team:

- Make the distinction between rules of the house and serious disciplinary matters
- Household rules apply across the board. Because they apply to everyone, they are non-personal. As already

discussed, a step-parent should have enough confidence
to ask that these rules be respected
- Discipline is a different ballgame. It is a personal remedy,
  tailored to suit the wayward individual
- Whenever possible, it is advisable for the parent rather
  than the step-parent to enforce discipline. A mother or
  father stands on the firm ground of biological parenthood,
  which minimises resentment
- However, a couple should make it clear that a step-parent
  does have authority in the home. When a step-parent is
  compelled to take sole charge he or she needs to be able to
  exercise control

Leisure Time

Family life is only enjoyable if all the obligations it imposes are
tempered with a strong dose of fun. This is especially true in the
case of stepfamilies, where these positive experiences have great
value in fusing old with new. If you can take pleasure in whatever
activity appeals to your stepchildren, you'll be well on the way to
creating an enduring bond.

Whatever it is that you can do together, from biking to shopping,
cooking to rock-climbing, it presents you with an opportunity to
hang out with the stepchildren on the same level, where you lose
your status as an authority figure and become simply someone
who wants to enjoy yourself. In this context, you are no longer perceived as a grim step-parent but as someone much more
approachable.

When at home, however, stepchildren have particular ideas
about how they want to spend their free time. These may or
may not correspond with your ideas. Step-parents frequently
fall into the trap of being critical, wondering what on earth they
have in common with their stepchildren, or indeed whether
their stepchildren are from Planet Earth at all. The fact that your

stepchildren do not share your interests does not however make them into aliens.

A live-and-let-live philosophy is necessary here. Sometimes you will be doing stuff together and feeling the positive consequences of this collective engagement. But there will be other times when everyone retreats into their own interests. It's up to you and your partner to get the emphasis right.

- Hobbies, activities, watching television, listening to or playing music, and computer games all come under the heading of personal entertainment. The issue of whether or not these types of personal entertainment need regulating must be determined by both parent and step-parent. If one of you has very strong feelings these must be taken into account and a compromise reached. Try to avoid being railroaded into allowing what you both consider to be excessive, as this only leads to resentment
- Balance leisure time spent independently with activities that you can all do as a family
- Plan things you can do as a family, whatever appeals to all of you: adventure parks, museums, going out for a meal, walking, playing games, watching a film
- Getting out of the house and being all together somewhere different from your home patch is often a positive experience, encouraging everyone to leave some stepfamily baggage behind. Prioritise outings of this kind so that they become a regular part of your stepfamily routine. It's worth making the effort, even with grumpy tots and taciturn teenagers. And it creates a bank of good memories that you all share
- Be as flexible as possible when it comes to trips. Although some trips need planning, it's good to be spontaneous too. A suggestion from a stepchild, no matter how goofy-sounding, should not be discounted

- Taking photographs/family videos which can be viewed at a later date, or given to stepchildren or put up about the house, all adds to the sense that you are a unit
- Don't slide into thinking that you must always do everything together. Vary the dynamic: it can be advantageous for a parent to be with his/her children without the step-parent once in a while
- Also, when a step-parent is ready, going on solo outings with the stepchildren can be healing too. Do something that you are comfortable with, where you'll feel relaxed, and this will rub off on the children

Stepchildren's Birthdays and Other Family Occasions

These markers in the calendar year offer great opportunities for demonstrating good will. Regardless of your actual sentiments for your stepchildren, birthdays and other festive days give you the chance to present your best step-parenting side. Let your partner help you to realise this objective.

- Expectations about birthdays are difficult to contain, particularly for young children. Adult stepchildren are not immune to their own birthdays either
- Forget any negative feelings that you may be harbouring. Preparing for a birthday raises the possibility of redressing the balance and showing your commitment to your stepchildren
- Get the right mindset here: the emphasis is on the effort you put in, not on the feedback you get. Imagine a scenario where the present you have so carefully chosen is hardly registered by your stepchild. Take that as your bottom line. But do not be deceived by appearances. No matter what they say or fail to say, they will be impressed and grateful deep down. Part of skilled step-parenting is

learning to distinguish between what the stepchildren can express and what they cannot. Don't lose sight of the fact that they may not be *able* to thank you adequately or at all. Remind yourself that this deficiency is perfectly natural and it is also fine by you

- Even if you are suffering from a little hurt pride, force yourself to be the grown-up and indulge a hostile stepchild
- Lavishing affection in the form of a baked cake, a decorated room, a party or a special present is a fantastic way of indicating that no matter what has happened in the past you are committed to a better future together
- Relish these windows of opportunity because normality will be restored tomorrow. Birthdays are one-offs which can make your stepchildren reassess what they think about you. So go on, give them some food for thought!

Holidays

Children and adults alike enjoy throwing some kit in a case and heading off to pitch camp somewhere different for a week or two. The prospect of a holiday conjures up visions of temporary bliss. Squaring reality with these dreams is a fraught business, especially in stepfamilies.

If your stepchildren live with you, being together full-time on holiday is nothing unusual, though of course travelling is a more intense version of everyday life, given that nobody takes a break to go to school or work.

If your stepchildren are non-resident, taking them off on a break is likely to be both challenging and rewarding. For once, you can all relax into a proper rhythm of being together. However, being unfamiliar with twenty-four/seven step-parenting can mean that the novelty quickly becomes a strain.

In short, stepfamily holidays are about getting the balance

right. On the one hand there's everything you ever dreamed of, both in terms of ideal getaways and ideal stepfamily interaction. On the other hand there is the black-and-white reality of how well you actually get along and what kind of holiday is genuinely feasible in the circumstances. With a little work, the pair of you can devise something appropriate for all. Keep the following pointers in mind:

- Don't be over-ambitious first time around. Plan a short break just to test the waters
- Choose a format that includes ingredients for the stepchildren as well as yourselves – going trekking when they hate walking is a bad idea, for example
- Going to the other extreme and choosing somewhere that has no adult appeal is also asking for trouble
- Once you've found a good compromise, get to work on your expectations. Your determination to enjoy your holiday may not be matched by your stepchildren's. Be prepared for your ideal holiday to be brought down to earth by sulky or uncooperative stepchildren
- Remember that there is a benefit in simply being away together, no matter what the behaviour of your stepchildren. This may not be the best holiday ever, but it's a vital training ground, giving you all an opportunity to work through some of your differences and come out stronger as a result
- A foreign environment can be disorientating for children, possibly making them feel more insecure than usual, which can tip into other forms of unrewarding behaviour
- Analyse the emotional requirements of your stepchildren: do they need a little time alone with your partner, or to speak to their absent bioparent? Do not however feel obliged to be over-indulgent. Stepchildren can sulk intermittently, but should not be allowed to rain on the

whole parade. Even stepchildren with painful issues can make some effort some of the time

- Try to create an atmosphere that makes a reluctant stepchild actively want to join in with whatever you have planned. This approach enables much of the step-parent–stepchild power struggle to be put to one side
- Once again, if you are experiencing step-parenting angst, get into the habit of taking a little time out. If your partner is around, engineer a moment where you can vent some of your own frustrations and make sure that he or she gives you a little positive feedback and reassurance.
  Alternatively, take yourself out of the equation, retreat into solitude and calm yourself down. Nobody said being a step-parent was easy

Repairing Rifts in Your Partnership

Inevitably there will be times when you and your partner do not see eye to eye. There is no getting around the differing perspectives of parent and step-parent. Despite the best will in the world, harmony cannot be the order of the day, every day, when it comes to running a stepfamily.

Most arguments have their roots in small, seemingly irrelevant incidents that happen as part of the daily routine. This is the kind of dispute that we are focusing on here. More profound fractures need specialist attention and are the province of marriage counsellors. But low-level disagreements can be resolved at home, provided that you are both able to turn a critical eye on your own behaviour.

The fact that most rows have trivial beginnings is not enough to prevent escalation. It's embarrassing the way these tiny troubles can get distorted into a monumental conflict. Who gets the butter from the fridge can become a matter of life and death.

Keeping a sense of proportion is a vital tool for both parties at the helm of a stepfamily. Even when you feel cast out, your partnership has enough strength to reel you back in. Be aware of the discrepancies listed below. Turn a critical eye on yourself, make sure your partner does the same, and talk it through until you both understand what went wrong and where.

Step-parents tend to	Parents tend to
1. Care too deeply about whether or not household policy is being followed	1. Be more relaxed about the observance of house policy
2. Forget that it's better to try to give their stepchildren some space	2. Be critical of the step-parent's high tension levels
3. Be critical of their partner's indulgent attitude towards his/her kids	3. Indulge the children at the expense of indulging the step-parent
4. Block out the awful truth that they are jealous of this strong parental love	4. Not realise that a step-parent is feeling excluded
5. Feel inadequate because they cannot match the depth of parental love, which in turn can lead to guilt	5. Be blind to the struggles of the step-parent to find his or her step-parenting identity
6. Believe that the stepchildren are spoiled and that this makes life more tricky for the step-parent	6. Equate love with never depriving their offspring of what they want
7. Harbour feelings that they have not been properly consulted/thanked/appreciated	7. Provide insufficient support when being a step-parent can seem a thankless task

8. Bury feelings of resentment instead of expressing them to their partner

8. Be dismissive instead of listening and responding

9. Forget that they have a valuable and key contribution to make to stepfamily life

9. Have trouble allowing the step-parent their proper place in the stepfamily

All couples disagree with each other now and then. The trick is not to invest these disagreements with extra emotion. When you've had a row, go through the above checklist and highlight which of the nine misunderstandings most accurately describes the argument. Use this to rethink your approach – not on your own, but as a couple.

Protecting Your Partnership

As with any long-term couple, what ties the pair of you together cannot be taken for granted. Putting a premium on safeguarding your relationship is particularly important when one of you is a step-parent. The stepfamily structure is imbalanced, as one of you struggles to maintain self-esteem in what is frequently a gruelling environment.

Fundamental to the first cornerstone is the understanding that your partner has to compensate for this imbalance by being unstintingly generous when it comes to looking after you. This is all part of the stepfamily bargain: you make your partner happy by working hard to keep things running smoothly with his or her children, and in return you need to have fun just the two of you, to be fussed over and indulged.

The psychologist James Bray observed that there was a lack of 'honeymoon effect' in remarried couples.[4] First marriages are often imbued with a romantic sense of pioneering, as the couple grows into new experiences together. But when one of you has been through these experiences already, and the other has not, it's difficult to recreate that same sense of romantic endeavour. Provided that a couple is aware of this, action can be taken to ensure the health and happiness of your bond.

Practical Exercise

This is an exercise that you and your partner do together. The aim is to check that as a step-parent you feel fully supported by your partner.

1. Does your partner acknowledge that being a step-parent places a special burden on you?
2. How is this acknowledgement communicated? Directly or indirectly? Verbally or by other means, special gifts, privileges and gestures of appreciation?
3. Discuss the basics of this process: do you feel sufficiently appreciated by your partner? Does your partner find it easy to honour all your hard work? Check that you are getting enough support and that your partner realises the need to keep the support tank topped up at all times

6

Stepfamilies Across the Spectrum

Any given stepfamily consists of a few select characteristics out of a long list of possibles. The straightforward structure of an intact family is replaced by a long list of variables. Different routes towards formation, different experiences depending on gender, age and parental status of the step-parent, as well the individual complexity of the units they are joining go some way towards explaining the massive range of stepfamily types.

Stepfamilies can be classified along a number of lines: the step-mother/stepfather divide, the custodial/non-custodial divide, the distinction between stepsons and stepdaughters. There are other variables to consider and, as the classification grows in complexity, a picture is drawn of each stepfamily.

There is however one axis that is reserved for a later chapter and this is the reason for the disintegration of the original family unit. Whether the family of origin came undone through divorce or death is the starting point for Chapter 10: The Ex Factor. This distinction governs a step-parent's relationship with his or her biological counterpart, which is a live issue even when that person has in fact died.

The Gender Divide

The nature of your dealings with your stepchildren is heavily influenced by whether you are a stepfather or a stepmother.

Stepfathers

Settling down with a woman who has children from a previous relationship is 'not something that any of us ever imagine', as one stepfather told me. When confronted with this situation, men can usually rely on the tried and tested role of main breadwinner. This gives them instant value, as they make a recognisable and important contribution. The new stepfather can be 'welcomed into the family unit as a saviour. Before his arrival, that family could have spent a long time being financially and emotionally bereft; the mother feeling lonely and unloved. The children may also welcome a stepfather, as long as his introduction into the family unit had been sensitively handled.'[1]

This is not to say that stepfathers are immune from provoking resentment. Many children feel jealous of the amount of attention that their mother now lavishes on her new husband. The mother may become 'less physically and emotionally available' to the child, who may experience feelings of anger and rejection.[2] The new partnership provides a remarried mother with an alternative focus, and probably she also feels indebted to her partner for helping out financially.

Stepfathers define their position in the stepfamily primarily in relation to their partner. They 'tend to see their role as to provide material and emotional support to the mother'.[3] Men prioritise the bond with their partner and think of this as their principal obligation, partly because 'society is not quite sure what role a stepfather should fill, other than to be the main financial support. Men are on the whole, less involved in the raising of children.

Even in natural, nuclear families, the father can be a distant, shadowy figure in children's lives.'[4]

However most stepfathers live with their stepchildren full-time as it is usually the mother who has custody of her offspring. Living in such close quarters necessitates a degree of interaction. And because a man in such a situation is not offered any clear guidelines as to how to behave with his stepchildren, he may well fall back on the easy option: law enforcement.

Discipline is perhaps the area of greatest conflict for the stepfather and his stepfamily. According to *The Reconstituted Family*, 'Many men who lived with their wife's children felt the wife was too lenient and didn't discipline her own children sufficiently.'[5] Problems are often amplified by a mother's confusion on this issue: 'Many men cite their wife's vocal insistence that she would like more help disciplining her own children, only to rebuff him when he tries. If stepfathers get the issue of discipline wrong, it can cause terrible angst for the children and the mother.'[6]

All the evidence points to a single conclusion: a child will only accept discipline from an adult with whom they have a close relationship. Pitching up and immediately releasing a volley of reprimands is a recipe for disaster that achieves nothing except universal frustration. Most step-parents, men and women, have the impulse to weigh in before any positive bond has had a chance of taking root. Often things are said on the spur of the moment and only thought about afterwards. This was very much the experience of another stepfather interviewed, who said:

Sometimes Penny and I would have discussions about the fact that I waded in a bit too early and a bit too enthusiastically into this whole business of telling them what to do. I'm a bit of a bossy git but I've dropped that a whole lot now. But you know, my wife appreciated the extra help in one way. She said that while she'd been a single mother there were so many things to worry about that fretting about the kids' table manners was just not a priority.

Others however are less quick to take the initiative with their stepchildren. A stepfather can be 'reluctant to put himself forward as part of the team providing a child's primary care'.[7] It can take a while for a stepfather to embrace the reality of his stepchildren on both a practical and an emotional level.

There is a widespread social prejudice that children and parents should share the same surname. A child will not have the same name as their stepfather, and the mother may make things worse by opting to take her new husband's name. Many stepchildren 'find the difference in surnames an embarrassment'.[8]

Yet a stepfather is often reluctant to get involved with his or her stepchild's education, and this cannot be explained purely in terms of different surnames. Nor can it be attributed entirely to the disparaging take of many schools towards step-parents in general. It appears that stepfathers as a breed are not overly concerned in their stepchild's schooling, with 33 per cent showing 'little or no interest'.[9] Children with stepfathers have poorer records than stepmother families when it comes to school attendance and are more likely to have been in contact with an educational welfare officer.[10]

However, once stepfathers have sweated through the initial phase of adjustment, which typically takes between eighteen and twenty-four months, he becomes a fully integrated and valued member of the stepfamily to a greater extent than even he may have envisaged. This was demonstrated in one study which revealed the degree of 'self-inflicted pressure' that stepfathers subjected themselves to.[11] In other words, stepfathers tended to be much more critical of their performance than natural fathers, even though these criticisms were in no way backed up by the other members of their stepfamilies.

Overall, stepfathers 'are necessarily a more distant element in a stepchild's life'. It all comes down to the expectations of society with regard to men and women. Because men are allowed to take more of a back seat in family life, they are 'less prone to conflict'[12] than their female counterparts.

Stepmothers

What we expect of women and what as a consequence women expect of themselves is arguably more complex, demanding and well-nigh impossible to achieve. This is only one of the reasons for the fact that stepmothers find stepfamily life more problematic than stepfathers.

The conclusion that women experience more difficulty with their step-parenting identity than men is reached in numerous studies, from the early days of Bowerman and Irish in the 1960s[13] to present-day research. 'Society expects the mother to be the main source of nurture and affection in a child's life, whether it is her natural child or not'.[14] Even in this post-feminist era, the belief that women are driven by their biological imperative is still common currency. This imperative includes not only reproduction but also protecting and caring for the young. These assumptions are woven into every layer of our culture, conditioning each new generation to subscribe to the same values. Unfortunately, such entrenched attitudes are directly responsible for much of the trauma that many women experience as they begin their lives as stepmothers.

The truth is that women are laden down with unnecessary and troublesome baggage when it comes to dealing with their stepchildren, and men are frequently unwitting accomplices here. 'Many natural fathers look to the wife and stepmother to smooth over family tensions. The wife often expects this too, which is unrealistic and often ends in conflict.'[15] Instead of assessing the particular characters of the kids involved, a woman is more than likely to be armed with her own agenda, that of the home-maker, nurturing and healing with one hand as she irons and cooks with the other. It is an unbelievably tall order and wildly unrealistic too.

Is this really what youngsters want from Daddy's new girlfriend? Do they want someone to fuss over them and tell them how they look and what to eat? With the best will in the world, a stepmother can easily go overboard precisely because of the conditioning she has been exposed to, toiling away on behalf of her partner and stepchildren as if this is the only plausible way of being.

Although the role of stepmother can be negatively defined as not being a natural mother, what is there in the way of positive guidance? We receive contradictory signals here. 'Society expects stepmothers to not act as parents yet love their children as their own.'[16] No wonder that we slide into confusion and stress. Stepmothers have a high incidence of anxiety, depression and anger as a result of these cultural mixed messages.[17]

Inadvertently women set themselves up for rejection, working hard and hoping that in doing so they will earn the affection, gratitude and ultimately love of their stepchildren. They have trouble recognising that their primary bond is to their partner and that this is sufficient justification for their presence in the household. Women tend to adopt a more holistic approach to stepfamily life, wanting desperately to be included within the family group, to be indispensable to everybody.

But the majority of stepmothers do not live full-time with their stepchildren, who usually remain with their biological mother, and this greatly reduces their need to be clucked over by their dad's new mate. Getting to know each other is a process that is quite separate from the caregiver and cared-for dynamic, although many of us fall into the trap of thinking that these two distinct issues are the same thing.

However the parameters change for custodial stepmothers, who are part of the team providing a child's primary care. Miriam Stoppard told me how she had wrestled to understand the limits of what she should be for her two stepsons, who came to live with her and her husband at the ages of two years and nine months, saying:

I felt that I was treading on eggshells, I really did. I was determined not to replace their mum in any way, and so I set out to just be their friend, but they were so little that this made a mockery of all my intentions. I desperately wanted to be liked by them and kept holding back from setting boundaries just in case that made them go off me.

I was at my wits' end, exhausted and at a loss about how to continue when my approach obviously wasn't working. One day I explained the problems that I was having to my husband, and he said, 'Listen, don't pussy-foot around. You're in charge!' After that I woke up and got on with the job. After all these little boys did need a lot of looking after.

Women in this situation seem to acquit themselves very well indeed, taking on full responsibility for their stepchildren's welfare and education. One report stated that stepmothers took an active interest in the schooling of their stepchildren, who were just as likely to do well as children from unbroken families of origin[18] and have an excellent record when it came to school attendance. The report went on to observe that stepmothers frequently surpassed the levels of concern shown by remarried natural mothers in their own biological children from a previous relationship.

Stepmothers tend to have problems in relation to their partner's ex-wife, as further discussed in Chapter 10. This is unfortunate, as these issues often become an obstacle to contact. It is a sad fact that in the majority of cases where a non-custodial father has remarried, access to his children suffers a body-blow.

Often, following remarriage, the relationship between an absent father and his children withers,[19] sometimes dwindling down to absolutely nothing, which is a tragedy for both parent and child. 'Good relations and frequent contact with non-resident fathers is linked to better adjustment in both boys and girls', states Marilyn Ihinger-Tallman, the leading expert in the field.[20] Instinctively we all know this to be true, as kids need the input of both a mother and a father. Today there are a number of active, vocal groups that publicise the plight of the father denied access to his children, such as the British organisation Fathers 4 Justice.

The blame lies with both parties in the new marriage. It's all too easy for a wife to claim that contact is nothing to do with her, but if she finds it stressful dealing with her stepchildren then she may subconsciously create an environment in which her husband feels less able to include his children, and they in turn feel marginalised as a result. It is part of a stepmother's obligation to facilitate a child's relationship with their father, even when this causes considerable personal stress. It's only through regular, frequent interaction with her stepchildren that a woman can overcome these teething problems. What seems like the easy option, namely ducking out of the situation entirely, does nothing but exacerbate a stepmother's difficulties in the long run.

The difficulty of a woman's task is linked to the age of the children at the time she became their stepmother. All the evidence suggests that pre-adolescents find it easier to accept their father's new partner than teenagers.[21] Pre-schoolers have the least difficulty of all.

This same study acknowledged that the age of the stepmother is another influential factor in the make-up of a stepfamily. It appears that stepmothers who were forty or above had a higher chance of a successful relationship with their stepchildren, at 70 per cent, compared to women under forty, of whom only 52 per cent estimated they had excellent relations with their stepchildren.

It's worth mentioning the cult of the wicked stepmother, adverse propaganda which is drip-fed into the minds of the smallest kids. Such considerable prejudice can be difficult to overcome, as one writer observed in this overheard remark of a young child:

'Is that your stepmother?'

'Yes.' (After a pause): 'Oh. I always thought a stepmother was something like a witch.'[22]

Perhaps this also helps to explain why women have more trouble with their step-parenting identities than their male counterparts.

The Step-parent Without Biokids/ Step-parent With Biokids Divide

When it comes to interacting with stepchildren, opinion is divided over whether being a biological parent as well is an asset or not. Being a bioparent provides useful experience, of course, but it also ushers in a stark contrast between the absolute nature of the blood tie and the more ambiguous nature of the relationship with the stepchildren. Arguably, non-parents fare better with their stepchildren precisely because they lack this comparison.

Step-parents Who Are Not Biological Parents

In the step-parenting community, the single group that has the fewest problems is stepfathers who are not already biological fathers. Here 'the stepfather can relate to the stepchildren more as natural children. They do not carry with them guilt at having left children of a previous marriage, and can therefore relate more clearly and easily to their stepchildren. Also, with no other children to deal with there are no conflicts over separating out different value systems.'[23]

Interestingly, the same does not hold true for women. A step-mother who is not a biomother tends to have more difficulties than step-parents with children of their own. Often this is because she lacks confidence when it comes to caring for youngsters. But it also comes back to the question of how women find validation. A woman who has not produced her own biological children invests a great deal in the idea of loving and being loved by her stepchildren, as described by Delia Ephron:

Lisa and Alex were leaving for camp. We were at the bus. All of us: the children, their father, their mother and me. It was the perfect picture of the 1980s family – three parents seeing two children off to camp. Larry was making sure the kids had pre-stamped and -addressed envelopes so they would write. Their mother was hunting for the camp nurse to give her Alex's antibiotic. I stood there holding a packet of M&Ms for each, thinking, I'm going to be kissed goodbye last.

It crosses my mind, as I write this, what a pathetic, whiny little thought that was. My husband and his ex-wife were getting on with the business of parenting, and I was thinking about me. How much am I loved? And, assessing the situation accurately, I concluded, 'Less.'

Of course, less. Less is appropriate. So why was I standing there reminding myself, feeling yet again sorry for myself?[24]

When it comes to being a step-parent, the absence of biological children can be a benefit for a stepfather, whereas for women it can be something of a complication. However, generalisations on this level often break down when it comes to the individual case.

Step-parents Who Are Also Biological Parents

Stepfamilies are at their most complex when combining children from two or more relationships. Reconciling the differing attitudes of bioparent and step-parent is a real feat. A natural parent has a built-in level of acceptance for his or her offspring which does not necessarily extend to a stepchild. What is manifestly clear is the importance of being even-handed; the bioparent and step-parent must make this a priority. It's not just a case of being fair, but also of being seen to be fair. The perception of equality is essential, as one such stepmother explained:

Paul and Stephen came to live with us when they were eight and five, and by that stage my boys were four and two. I worked really hard to treat them all just the same. And because my stepchildren were a little at sea, I over-compensated by coming down on my own kids harder than I did on either Paul or Stephen. Over the years, this led to a lot of complaining from my pair of nippers, who bleated endlessly that I wasn't being fair. My kids said that I was always quick to jump down their throats when I let my stepsons off the hook.

This woman did her level best to treat her biochildren and stepchildren as equals, but despite the best will in the world, combining the two roles of step-parenthood and natural parenthood is an enormous challenge. After the above interview, I went on to talk to the stepson Paul, who saw the past from a different perspective:

It was really, really hard for Stephen especially. I was OK because my half-brothers looked up to me. But Tom, the four-year-old had a weaselly streak. He's always liked to push people's buttons and this is what he did to Stephen when I was away at school. He'd needle him in all sorts of ways, making him really unhappy.

Tom would jab Stephen ten times in the back before he [Stephen] walloped him one. Instinctively a parent thinks the little ones are at risk and more vulnerable but that wasn't true here. I adore my stepmother, still do, but this was something she just didn't see. In her eyes, Tom was always the victim. Blood's thicker than water and all that. It's such a shame because Stephen sort of closed down as a result. He became quite distrusting of people and still is to this day.

Anyone occupying the dual roles of parent and step-parent is well aware of the dangers of preferential treatment. Focusing on the specific needs of stepchildren when biological kids are in the picture is a feat of concentration,[25] and yet this is an essential part of our duty. Inevitably a step-parent, being as flawed as the next person, falls short of the ideal from time to time. But the determination to be flexible, inclusive and loving makes up for the occasional lapse in judgement. We cannot do more than rely on this as our guiding principle.

The Custodial/Non-custodial Divide

When a natural parent has custody of his or her children and subsequently settles down with a new partner, the unit that is formed is quite different from that of the non-custodial stepfamily. The stepchildren live full-time with their step-parent and everyone has much more of a chance to cohere as a group. When the stepchildren are only sometimes present, for visits, weekends and holidays, this part-time existence gives a different complexion to stepfamily life.

As a part-time stepmother, I am vaguely envious of the solidity that comes with custodial step-parenthood. There is a certain amount of turmoil created by the ebb and flow of coming together and dissolving time and again. But on the other hand, none of us stops being a step-parent just because our stepchildren are not around.

The Custodial Stepfamily

All stepfamilies are confronted with the same challenge of forging a new and binding family unit, and this, as we all know, takes time. Here the custodial arrangement clearly has an advantage; time is one commodity that is not in short supply when everyone is living under the same roof.

Frequency of interaction is a critical factor in the delicate growth of a new stepfamily. As Lucile Duberman remarked in *The Reconstituted Family*, 'The more people are with each other, the more they come to like each other. Thus, if the stepchild and the stepparent lived together, the chances were greater that they would become attached to one another.'[26]

However there is still a definite phase of adjustment for the stepfamily with resident stepchildren, which may be prolonged by absences as children go away to visit their other biological parent. This is only one of a host of reasons given by custodial biomothers for withholding contact as, superficially at least, this seems to contribute to a more harmonious atmosphere within the home.[27] Such restrictive attempts at fostering good stepfamily relations actually amount to a deprivation of a child's right of access to their absent parent. It's essential not to be short-sighted in this regard.

Most full-time step-parents are male, as courts favour granting custody to a natural mother. There are however a small percentage of custodial fathers[28] who 'have custody of their children after death or divorce. They have often formed a tight bond with their children, making it very difficult for the stepmother to enter into this clique. Fathers in this situation can have difficulty disciplining their children or allowing their new wives to do so either.'[29] The protective impulse of a single dad is akin to that of the lone mother, described in the previous section on stepfathers. Clearly allocating authority to a new partner is something of a trauma for a biological parent, regardless of gender.

The desire to be perceived as a 'normal' family is another custodial stepfamily universal; attempts are made to gloss over the reconstituted nature of their grouping. On this theme, one mother said, 'My husband likes nothing more than being told that his stepdaughter looks just like him.'[30]

Emily and John Visher expanded on this point: 'Many in step relationships lie on forms to conceal their, as they see it, shameful status. Members of stepfamilies also rarely respond to call-in shows about stepfamily problems or to workshops or lectures aimed specifically at them.'[31] This is perhaps a reflection not only of generalised social stigma, but also of a self-conscious attitude to former relationship breakdown. For most stepfamilies follow on from divorce and for at least one of the partners in the remarriage this represents failure.

For the greater part, custodial stepfamilies are thoroughly integrated, mutually supportive units. In one study, 70 per cent of full-time stepfamilies rated themselves as happy;[32] a heartening majority.

The Joint-Custody Stepfamily

Joint custody is relatively rare, as the logistics of dividing a child's time equally between two homes can be formidable. But the clear advantage of this arrangement is that a child grows up being continuously cared for by both biological parents.

However the repeated shuttling to and fro can breed its own stresses for both generations. 'If children are endlessly shifted back and forth, these children usually become disenfranchised' and can suffer from feelings of disorientation and possibly low self-esteem.[33]

The complications of negotiating hand-overs, dealing with the practical details of the children's welfare and sharing responsibility for their emotional well-being make joint custody quite an undertaking. Often a biological father only feels in a position to shoulder such an arrangement once he has remarried, as the new partnership creates a stable environment for raising children. And yet a biological mother can feel nervous at the idea of sharing custody, and can have her own difficulties adjusting to another woman providing maternal care.[34]

It appears that joint custody is difficult both to achieve and to sustain. Implementing such a system essentially requires an amicable relationship between the two separated parents. Technically this may seem a superfluous requirement, but in practice the high level of contact becomes a trauma unless the ex-spouses get along tolerably well.

There are instances where joint custody works beautifully, as one such stepmother explained:

> I think it works well because my husband has always been so hands-on with the kids – you know, he did the main bulk of the daytime childcare when he was married to his first wife and so the pattern was already there. When they split up, things never got nasty. In fact, it was pretty civilised and that helped.
>
> His children definitely like the two-homes business. Both houses are near each other. All their school uniform is kept at their mum's but it feels like their base for playing and holidays is our place. We're really lucky.

The Non-custodial Stepfamily

When stepchildren live somewhere else and are only intermittently part of your household, it is extremely hard to establish continuity between one visit and the next. Inevitably these visits have an intense quality as the non-custodial parent has only a short period in which to demonstrate the strength of his or her commitment to the children.

Because contact between non-custodial parent and child is restricted, times that are shared become emotionally charged. Both parent and child are under pressure to condense the entirety of their relationship into a weekend, a holiday or occasionally just an afternoon. In practice, this often leads to the non-resident child being over-indulged.

Most non-custodial parents are fathers who 'preferred not to discipline the children because they wanted to use the visitation time for recreation, love and strengthening the relationship'.[35]

Guilt can be a major factor here. If a father is burdened by a sense that he has let his children down, this influences the quality of the time spent together. If things are 'strained, feelings of guilt and rejection increase and impinge on the happiness of the father and those around him'.[36] Sometimes a non-custodial parent compensates by lavishing a child with money and presents, and this can ruffle the feathers of a new partner and any children who do live under their roof.

Visiting stepchildren are likely to be only too aware of their transient status within their non-custodial stepfamily. Although they are nominally included all the time, in reality they are only partial members of their second home. This truth can be awkward for all concerned, as the adults strive to create a sense of belonging for the important visitors, wanting them to put down some roots, keeping toys or clothes or books in their room to demonstrate that this is their home too. But children can be resistant to this policy, as one stepdaughter was quick to point out to me:

> Dad and Christine made an enormous effort to make us feel that their house was as much a home as our mum's house. We'd go there for the weekends, and did keep our clothes there, but they were different clothes and it was sort of weirdly like having two lives.
>
> Don't get me wrong – I really appreciate the efforts that were made, but in retrospect I think that what they were trying to do wasn't realistic or possible. I mean you can feel at home somewhere but that's very different to feeling that it *is* your home. I knew that Dad would be upset if I referred to Mum's house as 'home'.

This girl's story is quite explicit about the stresses of an existence that is split between a full-time mother and a part-time father. It can be frustrating to watch everything being siphoned off to a child's principal home, but at the end of the day if this is what a stepson or stepdaughter needs to do, they should be allowed the freedom to do it, even if it leaves a rather empty-looking bedroom. My own stepdaughters got round this problem by plastering posters all over their bedroom in our house, making it very much their space despite the absence of other stuff, which they prefer to bring and take away every time they stay.

We worked hard to cultivate a sense of their permanent belonging but these two girls are nobody's fools. The older one once expressed regret at being something of an ornament to a family that is always chugging along, whether they are there or not. This is an obvious down-side to the non-custodial situation, compensated for by extra attention on the girls when they are with us.

It can be tricky reconciling the everyday attitude towards a full-time child with the indulgent approach of an absent parent towards the part-time child. The arrival of stepchildren impacts on established routines and this can cause a degree of anxiety and upset all round.

An absent parent is largely dependent on the primary carer when it comes to arranging contact. The non-custodial father is sufficiently worried about maintaining contact with his kids that he often finds it hard negotiating with his ex-wife, who frequently gets to dictate the terms. This again causes annoyance in a new partner, who resents her lack of vote when it comes to making arrangements.

And yet despite the topsy-turvy life of the non-custodial stepfamily, there is every likelihood that a sense of cohesion will eventually develop. It just takes longer, is more liable to ups and downs and involves the co-operation of the primary carer.

Stepfamily Components

Stepdaughters

There is evidence to suggest that a child is more affected by the remarriage of a parent when that parent is of the same sex.[37] Consequently the arrival of a mother's new partner is of enormous consequence to a daughter, who tends to identify strongly with her mum.[38] One study indicated that the presence of a stepfather was a more significant factor in the delinquency of girls than in boys, who were less likely to point to their stepfather as being a complicating factor in their lives.[39]

Typically, after a certain age daughters assume a modicum of responsibility in the household and this is taken away from them when a man inserts himself into the home, as one woman told me:

> I was thirteen when my stepfather moved in and from being someone who played quite an active role, helping Mum look after my three younger brothers, I was suddenly put back in my box and treated like a stupid kid. It left me smarting and actually soured things with my stepfather for quite some time.

Although the turmoil that can explode between a stepmother and stepdaughter is legendary, it would appear that the overall impact of a stepmother is less profound than that of her male counterpart.

This is not to undermine the explosive quality of possessive daughters, who 'appear to be extremely competitive with their stepmothers for their father's affections'.[40] As mentioned above, girls tend to identify with their mothers and are quick to claim their father as part of their mother's territory. And personally I can testify that this leads to all sorts of complications.

Stepsons

Following the breakdown of his parents' relationship, a boy is quick to take on the mantle of 'man of the house', given that in the majority of cases it is the mother who has custody of the children.[41] As with his sisters, sons can feel displaced by the arrival of a 'new boyfriend, who is seen as a direct rival for their mother's affections'.[42]

Because boys identify with their fathers, adolescent males in particular often displace the anger they are feeling towards their biological father on to their stepfather. In other words, the new man of the house has to atone for the sins of the first man of the house. There is however an optimum age for a boy to acquire a stepfather and that is between five and eleven years old.[43]

According to the theory that a same-sex parent's remarriage is most upsetting, boys are more traumatised by the remarriage of their father than by their mother's remarriage. Yet this finding is offset by the realities of most divorce scenarios, where a child no longer lives full-time with his father and is often worried about a dad who may be living alone. In such circumstances, it may be possible for a stepson to welcome the arrival of a step-mother.[44]

Clinical research indicates that on balance stepsons have an easier relationship with their stepmothers than do stepdaughters, despite the fact that a stepmother signifies the remarriage of a boy's same-sex parent. The evidence that girls outstrip boys when it comes to antagonistic attitudes towards a stepmother can only be explained by the peculiarities of the fairer sex.

Half-siblings and Stepsiblings

When children from one relationship are forced to get along with a child produced by a different relationship, turbulence can follow. We witnessed this first-hand as one of my stepdaughters fought against the reality of her baby half-brother. As long as the baby remained a blob, she wasn't that bothered. But once the blob started walking, she wanted to run a mile.

The trouble was that our young son was so interested in this other child – wanting to play, to pat her, prod her and make friends. At breakfast, she would arrange the cereal packets in a large semicircle to block out the view of this gleeful toddler peering round the edge of the Weetabix. It seems funny now but it wasn't that funny at the time.

My stepdaughter's reaction was of course entirely typical. Taking on board a sibling from the same parental stock is hard enough. But a half- or stepsibling is quite different, whether this child has been produced with their parent or from the step-parent's previous relationship. Either way, it doesn't appeal.

Thankfully the long-term prognosis is positive. One American study of eighty-eight stepfamilies concluded, 'With few exceptions, the step-sibling relationships were tolerable, with 38% saying that they had "Good" or "Excellent" relations.'[45] As with the step-parent–stepchild dynamic, the process of adjustment is accelerated if everyone lives full-time under the same roof. Another similarity is the desire among step- and half-siblings to conform to the traditional ideal family, where all offspring are from the same genetic stock. Most stepchildren tidy up the edges of their stepfamily when it comes to presenting a public face, to quote a step-parent from Lucile Duberman's study above: 'The kids get along fairly well together. But when they are in public, they always refer to each other as brother and sister.'

Some further factors influence integration. The first is socio-economic status; when there's more money around, the tension levels drop and this affects the younger generation as well as the adults.[46] The second is the quality of the step-parent's relationship with his or her stepchild, which is an indicator of the overall quality of the stepsiblings' connection.[47] The age of the children is also of significance. It appears that older children have less trouble forming bonds with stepsiblings, and this is largely because they are more confident about setting and adhering to their own boundaries.[48]

Finally it is worth noting that the arrival of a half-sibling has great potential to bridge differences. Being related to the new baby, a stepchild may experience a greater sense of belonging to the new family and a heightened optimism. When the current partnership reproduce, a stepfamily becomes a 'blended' family, with children from a previous relationship vying for attention with the recent arrival. There is much evidence to indicate the long-term advantages of the blended familiy, but certainly teething problems crop up along the way.

Although the blended family is knitted together through kinship, enormous jealousy can erupt following the birth. One stepfather found his twelve-year-old stepdaughter packing her suitcase when his wife was in the hospital giving birth to their son, telling him rather tragically, 'I'm going to live with Auntie Sophie as you won't be needing me any more.'

It is of course threatening for a stepchild to confront an unfamiliar scenario, in which a new baby has two parents whereas he or she only has one (in the context of their stepfamily). Obviously their parent also appreciates this potentially painful fact, and feels protective of this child when arguments break out, which can be a pretty regular occurrence. It is a learning process for the stepfamily linchpin as much as for the children.

Grandparents

A stepfamily has the potential for three sets of grandparents:

1. *The step-parent's parents.* When their child marries someone who already has kids, parents are relatively even-handed towards these stepgrandchildren up until the time that the new marriage gives rise to children. The arrival of a natural grandchild can upset the applecart, as this stepfather told me in no uncertain terms:

I married Astrid when I was only twenty-six. She'd been left with daughters aged five and three, and her ex-husband had gone to live abroad. I never had any problems with her kids – they were fine with me. So pretty quickly, I did feel like they were mine. But my parents would never believe me. And it all came out of the woodwork when we had our own kids. Then their preference became impossible to ignore. I had to take my parents to one side, have a word, you know. It wasn't fair on the other two, it wasn't fair at all.

In stepfamilies, the question of inheritance can become fraught, and this was part of the problem in the above case history.

2. *The bioparent's parents.* Following the breakdown of their child's relationship, grandparents often help out in numerous ways, by supporting their child through the upset, looking after the children and generally providing continuity. This involvement is often curtailed by the arrival of a step-parent, who becomes an alternative source of support.

Feelings of displacement on the part of the grandparents can follow and this in turn affects their reaction to the new spouse. To quote Visher and Visher, 'Grandparents and grandchildren may form a tight unit to exclude all others. Destructive coalitions can occur in all types of families, but stepfamilies are at particular risk in this regard.'[49]

3. *The absent parent's parents.* When a child is in contact with his or her non-custodial bioparent, this person will usually be responsible for contact between his/her own parents and the child(ren). However, if a biological parent has died, contact with the deceased's parents will only be maintained through the stepfamily. In such a case, the obligation to continue the relationship is usually honoured by the stepfamily, as one stepmother in this situation explained:

My husband felt he owed it to Fiona's memory to keep up with her parents. So for years and years, every second weekend we would spend an incredibly boring half-day with them. We did this even when the children themselves were reluctant.

Occasionally their maternal granny would take them out. I still remember my shock and rage when she returned one day having taken Deedee to the hairdresser's and cut off her long, curly hair. And her granny simply didn't understand my thin-lipped reaction . . .

Blurring the Biological Boundaries: The Next Generation

What appears amazingly heartening is the testimony of many who grafted long and hard as step-parents and declared years later that their devotion to their stepgrandchildren was identical to their feelings for their biological grandchildren. The issues that characterise a step-parent's relationship with his or her stepchild do not get passed down the line. And that has to be a relief for everyone.

I'm already looking forward to the evening-out of the sometimes bumpy terrain that my natural and stepchildren inhabit. At some time in the future when our stepchildren reproduce, the equality of grandchildren is one of the many ways in which all our efforts are paid off.

7

The Second Cornerstone:
Know Your Role

Setting up home with someone who has children opens the floodgates to a tide of ideas about how you should behave as the step-parent. Like it or not, we are all driven by these ideas of not only what we should be but also how we should be received in this new and unfamiliar aspect of our lives. There are those who are keen to excel, those who are keen to stand back, those who need admiration and those who need order.

Whatever the individual predisposition, each and every one of us has an agenda when it comes to being a step-parent. But in subscribing to our own agenda, we are accidentally making our lives as step-parents ten times more difficult. If we give rein to our own idiosyncratic notions, we lose sight of a central truth: when it comes to our stepchildren, we come second.

Rationally every step-parent knows that a biological parent cannot be rivalled. In the beginning a step-parent is dominated by this awareness, as we lurk on the edges of their family life. But relatively soon, being only human, we focus increasingly on what we personally want out of this situation: to be included, to be liked, to be respected or whatever. Unfortunately, we focus on our own priorities at the expense of our original perception.

Without quite realising what is going on, a new partner sets about trying to secure his or her own objectives. This is understandable enough, given that he or she has to get comfortable in this unfamiliar stepfamily setting. But unless a step-parent turns a critical eye on these personal objectives, the situation can run into trouble very quickly. When we fail to achieve what we want, we are left seething and frustrated.

Most step-parents experience resentment to a greater or lesser degree. We find ourselves really minding about all the hard work we put in and about the lack of rewards we receive. We curse ourselves for being petty, for minding in the first place, but this does nothing to make the resentment go away. We have to make compromises, sacrifices even, that do not come easily. We have no time alone with our partner, who is so adored by these children whilst we are not.

In an effort to cope with all this negativity, we redouble our efforts and set about trying to realise whatever it is that is particularly important to us personally, whether that is winning the affection or approval or simple acceptance of our stepchildren, or the admiration of our partner.

This is our first big mistake. Inadvertently, we have fallen into believing that our position is only justifiable if our relationship with our stepchildren matches our views of what it should be. In other words, the whole stepfamily dynamic is reduced to a single issue: how are we faring with our stepchildren?

But this is to miss the point entirely. We are not in this situation because of our stepchildren. They most definitely did not invite us to be their step-parent. We are in this situation because of our union with their parent. *And this alone justifies our position.* We do not have to be loved and adored by the stepchildren; we do not even have to be liked by them. Nor do we have to prove ourselves to our partner by earning the affection of our stepchildren.

The only thing we have to do is help our partner deal with his or her kids, to facilitate the bond between parent and child as best we can. This is the only sensible definition of step-parenthood. We are not meant to be parents. To our stepchildren, we are something secondary and peripheral, an also-ran. This is the essence of our role.

We know that we are appreciated by our partner, as the first cornerstone established. This person is right there generously supplying endorsement, reassurance and love. And so we are given the strength to detach entirely from the emotional reactions of the stepchildren. We help look after them but we are not dependent on their reactions, as long as they can be vaguely civil. As step-parents, we are validated not by the unpredictable quantity that is our stepchildren, we are validated by our partners, who know that we are doing a great job helping out with the kids.

Accepting the limits of our role is an enormous relief. It frees us up from the greedy attitude of the desperate-to-be-appreciated step-parent that rapidly spirals into resentment. We are no longer at risk of injecting unnecessary emotions into what should be a straightforward business.

Once a step-parent stops obsessing about whether or not the stepchildren are sufficiently grateful, affectionate, warm or appreciative, we can appreciate that what the stepchildren feel about us is beyond our control. However, what we can control is our own approach. Be strict with yourself here: remember that in caring for your stepchildren you are in fact caring for your partner. It is a case of giving love in one direction and receiving love from quite another.

Sticking to this mindset can be truly liberating. The workload continues as before but it becomes less onerous. Tasks are carried out with a lighter heart. The liberated step-parent just gets on with the practical details and refuses to fuss about how he or she is perceived and whether sufficient thanks have been given. The liberated step-parent is content to focus on what he or she does have, which is the love and appreciation of their partner. Nothing has changed in terms of the situation, but your mindset has been transformed. Once you understand the basics of the step-parenting obligation, you can just get on with the job.

Eradicating resentment takes real, proper concentration. It is, like many things in step-parenting, an effort of will. Every time the urge creeps up to wail, 'It's not fair! I do so much and I don't even . . .' you must bite your tongue. The lot of a step-parent is neither fair nor unfair. It is our lot and we have to be adult enough to get on with it without sulking or self-indulgence.

Practical Exercise

Ask yourself whether you are counting the cost as you care for your stepchildren. This is the sinister beginning of what can develop into fully fledged resentment; a truly poisonous commodity.

The objective here is to monitor low-level frustrations and incipient bitterness. So whatever you are doing for your step-children, pick up your step-parenting record and ask yourself the following:

1. Do you expect more feedback than you actually receive? If so, what kind of feedback are you waiting for?
2. Ask yourself why you are feeling hard-done-by:
   do you want more affection or gratitude from the stepchildren? If so, correct your emphasis and look to your partner
3. Is your partner giving you enough support? If so, is there really a problem here?
4. Kicking the habit of expecting more rewards takes self-discipline. Pull yourself up short each and every time you feel like an unsung hero: being a grown-up means knuckling down and doing without the fanfare

5. Remind yourself that you are a great step-parent and that your efforts are fully appreciated by your partner

In falling in love with a parent, this is the deal we signed up for. By labouring for our stepchildren we are protecting our partnership and ensuring that our partner is happy. At the end of an exhausting step-parenting day, when you have disciplined your thought processes and avoided resentment, you will feel as proud of yourself as your partner is grateful for all your hard work.

Understanding the nature of our step-parenting identity can take a while. We are influenced by what we think is expected of us by society at large. The inclusion of the word 'parent' in our job description leads to all sorts of mayhem. We know that parents are bound to their children and are left wondering what binds us to our stepchildren; whether it is strong enough, affectionate enough or loving enough. A step-parent's task would be much easier if we were called something entirely different.

The Reasons for Role Confusion

One of you is the biological parent and the other expands to fill the void left by the other biological parent, or so the orthodoxy goes. Overnight, the fantasy hatches that the pair of you parent together. In fact this is far from the truth. Step-parents can be enormously loved and valued, adored by and indispensable to their stepchildren. But the relationship is still worlds away from the genetic link between natural parents and their off-spring. The step relationship is not inferior, just fundamentally different.

As a group, step-parents lack the confidence to carve out a niche for ourselves and for the relationship that we provide. According to a study in the *American Journal of Orthopsychiatry*, the stepfamily ought to be considered as 'a completely different child-rearing unit'. The study concluded: 'However strong the stepparent's determination to be a substitute parent, however skilful his efforts, he cannot succeed totally.'[1]

There are two reasons for this deep-seated misunderstanding of our role. Firstly, we are in partnership with someone who is the mother or father of our stepchildren, and being in partnership means doing things together. Secretly we long for the certainty provided by natural parenthood, hoping somehow to ride on our partner's coat tails.

The second reason is that, according to popular perception, there is only one model when it comes to family life: the intact union between two natural parents. We know exactly what to expect of a mother or father, and are immersed in stereotypes about earthy mums and inspiring dads. But as far as step-parents are concerned, the only stereotypes are negative, from Cinderella's wicked stepmother to Hamlet's malign stepfather.

There is a resounding lack of any positive role models for the step-parent, except perhaps Fräulein Maria in *The Sound of Music*, who arguably only won through because she could sing. Given that most of us don't charge through life armed with a guitar, we have nothing to fall back on but the tried and tested model of the traditional family. So we end up trying to adopt the familiar characters of a loving mother or devoted dad to these children who are at the outset total strangers. It is a recipe for disaster.

Why the Parenting Model Is Doomed to Fail

Unconditional love is something with which we are all familiar. We feel it for our own parents: an indissoluble chain that does not break even when contradictory personalities surface. The tie between parent and child is one of those extraordinary phenomena that nature has devised to protect the next generation. Natural parents are equipped not only with babies but with a programmed acceptance of their babies, ensuring a degree of tolerance of tots who draw on the walls, kids who pee on the carpet and teenagers who crash computers and cars. Natural parents have a strange capacity to roll with the punches when it comes to their own off-spring.

But step-parents do not have this capacity, and it's no good pretending otherwise. It's aiming too high to think that as a stranger we can even begin to approximate the responses of a mother or father. In flirting with the idea that we are something of a mum or dad to these kids, we are opening a can of worms.

Even the youngest children have a definite sense of their mum and dad. And when a child or a toddler is deprived of the truth, all hell can break loose. Robin was only eighteen months when his mother unexpectedly died. His story is extraordinarily painful and a lesson to us all:

Just over a year after my mother died, my dad found a new girl-friend. Rebecca was only twenty-three, not that I can actually remember any of this because I was only two years old.

The way Rebecca coped with it all was by deciding to become my mum, not just in a day-to-day way but in *every* way. And she worked hard to airbrush my real mother out of the picture, partly because she was jealous of my dad having this first wife, and partly because she didn't like the label 'stepmother' at all, she thought it sounded evil. But I say, if you don't want to be a step-mother, don't marry someone with kids.

Anyway, Rebecca was determined to fill a hundred per cent of the mother space. Basically, she came along and stole away the possibility of me remembering my mum in a relaxed way; it all became covert, hidden – almost dirty. Dimly perhaps I knew the facts but it was all repressed because we were never allowed to talk about these things.

So the truth became an explosive undercurrent, always hidden but always there. I ended up feeling like a fake, especially after she'd given birth to her daughters. It was like I had to go along with it, pretending she was a mum to me just as she was a mum to her girls.

Obviously Rebecca was taking on so much that she could never fulfil – she could never be my mother. She could only ever be a disappointment to me as a mother. And because there was always this conflict between what I knew to be true and their version of events, because my dad went along with it too, in my twenties I started having all these panic attacks and finally had a breakdown. Then at least things got spelled out . . .

As Robin observed, this woman 'could only ever be a disappointment to me as a mother'. This statement summarises exactly why we should take care: remodelling yourself as a mother or father is risking failure, not only for you, but for your partner and your stepchildren.

Role-blurring to this extent creates nothing but headaches for everyone, although each stepfamily member suffers in a different way from such confusion. It is worth examining each member in turn to be quite clear about the problems caused by the 'step-parent as parent' school of thought.

1. *The step-parent's adjustment.* The satisfaction of natural parenthood is a truism repeatedly reinforced by the media, politicians and society in general. We know that mothers and fathers are infinitely committed to their offspring. The hope sets in that by giving a solid motherly or fatherly performance, we too can match this level of commitment and satisfaction.

In relying on the gold standard of an idealised, all-forgiving parent, we can never make the grade. We compare our reactions to some kind of phoney, perfect parent and feel blameworthy and ashamed. By the same token, we feel guilty about almost everything we do and say – was this what a real parent would have done, said, allowed or forbidden? We curse ourselves for resenting our lot. Would a mother or father count the cost? No parent could possibly find caring for their child such a burden, could they? Therefore we brand ourselves a failure.

We know that real parents are rewarded with unconditional love. So we set about working tirelessly on the children's behalf in the hope of earning their gratitude, their affection and ultimately their love. But instead of being showered with thanks and praise, we are ignored, taken for granted or scorned. And so resentment sets in, as if the terms of this unspoken bargain have been broken not only by the step-parent, who is failing as a parent, but by the stepchildren, who cannot respond to them as a parent.

Give yourself a break and remember the primary reward of step-parenting. Nobody asked you to try to be a parent to these kids, but your partner did ask you to build a life with him or her. You're in this situation because you want to make your partner happy, not because you want to play mummies and daddies with your stepchildren.

In a successful partnership, each party prioritises the happiness of the other. If one half of the couple is a parent, he or she needs to discharge the duties of parenthood in order to be happy. In helping your partner to be a good father or mother to his or her children, you are looking after not only your partner but your partnership. This is the essence of step-parenting. The obligation is to the person with whom you share your life, not to your stepchildren.

Every step-parent needs to be self-disciplined on this score. We should keep a grip on the following principles which define our role:

- You understand the importance of your partner's relationship with his or her children
- Because you love your partner, you will do everything you can to make a success of your relationship with your stepchildren

- The care you provide for your stepchildren is a by-product of your union
- Thinking of yourself as a quasi-mum or quasi-dad will only get you into a muddle, leading you to expect too much from your stepchildren in the way of appreciation and affection
- Cut yourself off from wanting to be liked by your stepchildren. You are caring for them because of your obligation to make your partner happy
- You are in no way equivalent to a child's mother or father despite the unfortunate inclusion of these words in the job title of 'stepmother/father'
- Look to your partner for all the endorsement, validation and love that you need
- Just be yourself – this is after all the person your stepchildren will slowly come to accept
- Although you can never in a true sense be a parent, there is much that you can be for your stepchildren: an alternative source of support, encouragement, fondness, friendship and inspiration and ultimately love. This is the subject of the fourth cornerstone

2. *The parent's adjustment.* Before a stepfamily can be formed, the original partnership has to come undone. Relationships break down or a spouse dies, splintering the biological union that gave rise to your stepchild. Before you arrived on the scene, your partner was there, picking up the pieces of this fractured situation. As a single parent, whether custodial or non-custodial, he or she will have grown accustomed to shouldering the burden of looking after the children alone.

What this means in practice is that a single parent has to expand to fill both aspects of natural parenthood, with lone fathers expressing maternal attention to detail and lone mothers asserting their authority. Having weathered the storm of separation, a divorced or bereaved parent aims to provide all that a child needs in terms of emotional and physical care. And they are accustomed to doing this on their own, until we come along.

Coming into a pre-existing unit, a step-parent tends to wade in too deep and too quickly. In order to feel accepted, we need to feel important both to our partner and to his or her children. We are eager to prove ourselves in various capacities: as a great laugh, a fun person, a fantastic cook, a wonderful football coach; in short we are desperate to display all our good qualities so that we can gain admission into the very heart of this family. Because we are keen not only to be liked by our stepchildren but also to earn our partner's admiration, we charge ahead with all guns blazing. No wonder everyone runs for cover.

From managing perfectly well with his or her kids, a partner stares on in disbelief as we bustle about scratching out a job for ourselves and creating some kind of function that we can call our own. It's all too easy for a step-parent to lose sight of the fact that this unit was managing quite OK before we came along.

Accommodating a new partner into the family causes considerable anxiety to a parent (in fact, research has shown that all parents, male and female, find the issue of sharing authority with a partner causes stress). Given this, a step-parent should tread with care. It's not appropriate to bulldoze in, demanding to be a mother or a father to the stepchildren. It is disrespectful to the parent and to the stepchild.

3. *The step-child's adjustment.* Children have fixed ideas when it comes to their mum and dad. They want to be looked after by both parents, even in a post-divorce scenario.

Adults may find being a step-parent tricky, but arguably *having* a step-parent is even trickier. From a child's perspective the space around their mum is reserved for their dad, and vice versa. Once the family of origin disintegrates, a child struggles to adjust to this invasion of space reserved specifically for their absent parent. The fact that you are now standing right there, intimately connected with their mum or dad, is mighty difficult to process.

The difficulties increase in the custodial stepfamily, where a step-parent can end up actually shouldering more of the parenting work than an absent biological parent. A stepchild really struggles to come to terms with this new order. On one hand they rail against such an invasion, are threatened by it and resent an outsider's influence. But on the other hand, as they acclimatise and realise that their step-parent is actually providing quite a lot in terms of care or money or both, their conventional spirit creeps back and they may even acknowledge the benefits of the reconstituted family.

The conformist urge leads most children to experiment with the idea of the full-time step-parent as mum or dad. This often means dressing a step-parent up as a mummy or a daddy. Following a young child's logic, if you are part of the team providing a child's primary care, you must belong to the mum club or the dad club.

But the fluid mind of a child is quite able to embrace the reality of both biological parents and 'extra' parents, provided that the two are kept distinct. Miriam Stoppard recalls vividly how both her stepsons would chop and change on this issue:

When the boys first came to live with us, the older one was two and the other only nine months – they were so little that they did just call me Mum. My older stepson really wanted to sort things out in his head. He decided to call me by my first name because, as he said, 'Josie is my real mummy and I can't have two mummies, can I?'

That was fine by me, so for a while I was Miriam, but then I became 'Mum' again after he'd started school. He raced back home on the first day and said, 'Guess what? There's a boy in my class who's also got two mummies!' He was overjoyed, really relieved that he wasn't the only one, like he could suddenly relax.

The critical point is to allow a stepchild to take the lead here. It may well be that a child does need and want to call you Mummy or Daddy, but this initiative must come from them, not you. I spoke to one stepdaughter who had grown up furious with her stepfather's repeated claim that he was her father. This man was a public figure who was frequently interviewed on radio and television. 'It made my blood boil, it really did. He used to lump me and my sister in with his biological kids, declaring to the world that he had five children. And I had no right of reply, stuck at home seething whilst he was broadcasting all this private stuff over the airwaves.'

However, sometimes a child needs to use these labels, seizing on your potential to fill the slot, as happened with this stepmother:

When I met the twins, they were nearly five. Their mum had died when they were absolutely tiny. I'd been long-distance dating their dad and when I finally moved in I was very definitely Nancy. But the children were right on board from day one. When Douglas told them we were engaged, they were delighted, and ran around telling everyone, 'We're getting married!', which was fantastic.

I got closer to Harrison faster – he was the one who first called me Mummy. It was like he was trying it out just to test me, to see if he was going to get a response – if I was going to answer him. Andrew, the other twin, didn't like it all. He didn't understand. But Harrison just carried on, driving it home until finally, a month before the wedding, Andrew started calling me Mummy one time and Nancy the next. But pretty soon it became Mummy all the time.

But Douglas, my husband, has always made it clear to the boys that I am their mummy on earth and that they also have a mummy in heaven. We agreed that was the best way of explaining things. There's photos of her up in the house and that's cool. But it's a fine line, isn't it? We can't live in the past. We have to build our own traditions.

When a mother or father dies, a young child who has 'completed' his or her mourning is particularly willing to promote a step-parent to be Mum or Dad.[2] But most stepfamilies today come about not as a result of death but as the end-product of divorce.

When both bioparents are still alive, a child is keen to protect their separate identities, no matter where these parents happen to be. To avoid doubt as to who their biological parents really are, children of divorce here in Britain tend to call a step-parent by their first name when they're at home. In all my interviews of custodial step-parents, only 7 per cent were actually addressed as 'Mum' or 'Dad' by their stepchildren. This contrasts strongly with the American bias, which favours a step-parent being called 'Mom' or 'Dad' whenever possible.

Many British stepchildren refer to a custodial step-parent when they are out in public, with friends or at school as being their mother or father, despite preferring to call them by their first names in the privacy of their own home.

Clearly this is a complicated business for a child, and therefore we must do our level best to simplify our approach and remember that we are not and nor do we want to be parents; we are quite happy with our supplementary status. As one non-custodial step-mother to teenage stepdaughters told me, 'I hope that I am something of a bonus for my stepdaughters. They have a great mum who they adore. All I am is somebody else they can talk to, to look after them if they need it.'

The Fundamentals of Our Role

Having assimilated that our obligation is to our partner, not to our stepchildren, we can set about building on secure foundations. You are tremendously valued by your partner, who communicates this to you readily as set down in the first cornerstone.

In the context of your union, you and your partner are equals.

But when it comes to your stepchildren, the pair of you are most definitely not equals. So a step-parent comes second. As discussed at the beginning of this chapter, we are all aware of this in the early days. But as we settle into stepfamily life, we subconsciously fight against our subordination. Without realising quite what we are doing, we begin to resent our inferior status.

The truth is we don't want to come second to our partner. Our culture glorifies pole position, so we feel outraged that our stepchildren prefer their mum or dad. We are also outraged that our partner acquiesces in being preferred, and does not resign his or her superiority. We feel angry with everyone else for going along with the idea that it's fine to put a step-parent on a lower rung of the ladder.

Of course it is not only fine but inevitable that we are on a lower rung of the ladder. As soon as we crash back to earth and accept our inferior status as far as our stepchildren are concerned, we let go of the instrument of our pain.

For me this realisation was something of an epiphany. From yearning to be liked, loved even, by my stepdaughters, a craving that caused me endless misery, I changed tack and embraced my obvious inferiority. Yep, I was just a lesser mortal skulking about on the fringes of my stepdaughters' lives. When I served up lunch, cleared away supper, washed their hair or whatever, I no longer tried to quantify their gratitude. I'd stopped wanting their love. And the relief was unparalleled.

Equipped with this new mindset, I did all the chores as before but had a different way of experiencing the situation. It was like imagining the girls as random strangers passing through, rather than my stepdaughters. Of course I would look after them, as I would look after anybody who came to stay. But I refused to obsess about their responses or lack of them.

My transformed attitude had a remarkable knock-on effect on those around me. A pressure valve had been released and the atmosphere was revolutionised. The heavy climate created by my cloud of resentment had disappeared. It was easier to breathe, life was more relaxed. They could think what they liked about me, I didn't even mind if they thought I was their skivvy. In many ways I *was* their skivvy, but that didn't stop me from being my husband's equal.

With hindsight, I could see that an over-competitive spirit had caused me all sorts of problems. At the time, it didn't occur to me that the person I was being rivalrous with was in fact my husband. When caught up in a step love triangle, a step-parent is duped into thinking of the stepchildren as rivals. It can take a while to realise that we are in fact competing with our lover. The competition is ludicrous, the result a foregone conclusion. A step-parent would do much better sitting out this particular race. We should remember what we already have, which is the commitment and love of our partner.

Listed below are some of the manifestations of the urge to get to the top that topples many a step-parent. In knowing your role, you are less likely to suffer from any of the following egocentric tendencies:

The Paranoid Step-parent

The new step-parent is isolated – an outsider admitted into their partner's family. Being uncertain of how to proceed and doubting whether we should be there in the first place pushes us into insecurity. This is compounded by the ambivalence or downright loathing of our stepchildren, who clearly don't want us around.

Paranoia takes hold. We believe that we are in fact the aggravating factor here: if it wasn't for the bogeyman step-parent, everything would be fine. And so we blame ourselves for the whole situation.

The paranoid individual should give himself or herself a break. Wake up, take a deep breath and remember that a step-parent comes second. You did not cause this situation, you just fell in love with someone with kids. And the kids had their baggage long before you came on the scene, a truth which is at the core of the third cornerstone. You are not at fault here, assuming that you are doing your level best to facilitate your partner's relationship with his or her kids.

The Spoiled Step-parent

Children are by nature demanding, and parents are programmed to listen to their demands. Step-parents lack the programming to be so sympathetic to the endless stream of requests. Because we cannot rely on the same responses as our partner, we do not feel equally adult. This dilemma is neatly coined by the American author Delia Ephron: 'But in fact, as a stepmother, I am a child anyway. By default. Because in a family, if you aren't a parent, what are you?'[3]

Rationally we know we are adults, but stepfamily life can really reduce us to a mess of childish strops and tantrums. We cannot match the indulgent attitudes of our partners to these kids and this makes us feel inadequate. So we give up trying to be a grown-up altogether. Reason doesn't penetrate this state of mind, which is exactly what makes it dangerous in the extreme. In giving free rein to our neediness, we are at our most aggressive, concentrating entirely on getting what we want. It is not a pretty sight.

A spoiled step-parent may occasionally succeed in securing their desires but even when getting their own way, this person has no dignity. Despite being heard, such a step-parent is not respected. Low self-esteem is hot on the heels of such infantile behaviour.

Part of knowing our role is being able to accept calmly that we are outside the domain of the blood tie. In a first marriage, if you are not a parent you are a child. But now we have the wisdom to make a new model that applies specifically to the stepfamily. In this unit, if you are not a parent or a child, you are still an adult, quietly getting on with your own responsible business.

Accepting our identity is fundamental to successful step-parenting. Quash the slightest hint of babyish fury. Be a grown-up.

The Critical Step-parent

When we don't want to be left out, we get critical. We imagine that we know best, and we want our partner to know that we know best, so we tell them. Criticising is easy to do but it is not always easy to understand. Presenting our partner with an alternative that we consider superior is just another way of saying, 'Hey look, I can parent too – I'm just as good as you!'

It is a variation on a familiar theme: don't leave me out, let me in. In claiming that we know best, we are trying to outstrip our partner, to race ahead in a race we are not eligible to run. To quote Delia Ephron once again:

> I am utterly convinced that, were I this child's mother, I would never change my mind once it was made up. (Since I am not the child's mother, I am safe from ever finding out I'm wrong.) I regularly compliment myself with the thought, I'm much tougher than Larry is, and when given the opportunity I always prove I am. (Of course, I am – I'm the stepmother and not involved.) Right is on my side. Parents should set limits and stick to them – all psychologists agree with me. My friends all sympathize with my uphill struggle to whip my husband into shape. They know all about it because I complain to them regularly, 'Why doesn't he see what he's doing?' It doesn't temper my zealousness or make me more understanding to know that many divorced fathers are too indulgent, and there are reasons for it. I even know the reasons. They feel guilty about the divorce and are continually trying to make it up to their children by being nice. They are worried about losing their children's love, though, as all of us who read the psychology books know, children interpret limits as love. (Even when the daddies know this, their anxiety may make them unable to act on it.) And possibly some other reasons as well: laziness – it's easier to be nice than tough; misplaced generosity – the feeling that limiting your child is in some way being stingy; and inexperience as a disciplinarian. Being reluctant or too insecure to discipline your child is a sad situation to be in, but I am not saddened

by it because I am too busy trying to do something about it.

Larry always listens patiently to my pleas. He agrees with me. He's letting his daughter down. He must change. He will learn to be tougher. But why can't I shut up about it? Why can't I? No parent wants an unbiased observer in the house watching him. That is truly a parent's nightmare – at the least he should be allowed to screw up in private. And no one but a stepmother would think that a stepmother is unbiased. This is the tricky part. I may be right, but my motives are not what they seem.

To be as honest as possible, I sense not that I can't help but notice my husband's failings, but that a little part of me lies in wait for them. Is he going to change his mind? He does and I pounce. And behind all my helpful criticism is a needling, an implied 'If you won't follow my advice, who knows what will happen to your daughter!' I stir Larry up a little. It's a way of getting back at him for the fact that I'm not involved. Because despite whatever special perception the outside position gives me, I resent being there. In other words, I am an unbiased observer with a grudge.[4]

This is a refreshingly frank account of a tendency that many of us have experienced: we are at risk of overly interfering when it comes to our partner's children.

When push comes to shove, although we are in close alliance with our partners, ultimately we have to defer to them when it comes to their kids. Of course we have a vote but the right of veto belongs to our partner.

Earning the trust of a stepchild takes a long time, years in fact. To thunder about criticising your partner is dangerous enough; criticising a stepchild is potentially devastating. For a stepchild will rarely be able to stomach a step-parent's suggestion that they could do something differently or better. They have their own prejudices, which can be quickly turned back on, just when you thought you were over the worst.

The advice here is to stick to the ground rules that shape your stepfamily function. We should not invent new areas of personal expertise. Knowing our role means knowing our place.

The Authoritarian Step-parent

There are some of us who not only want to be heard but to be obeyed. Some incoming step-parents are at pains to demonstrate their authority. So the edicts begin to roll out: don't do this, do that, sit up straight, pay attention to the newcomer.

As with the critical step-parent described above, the disciplinarian's behaviour is just a different manifestation of the same muddled thinking about the limits of our role. Is a new stepfather meant to arrive and transform himself into Dad, enforcing law and order right, left and centre?

Barking reproaches at somebody else's kids is only appropriate once you have earned the trust of those kids. A new partner determined to be forceful is spurred on by the subconscious desire to be recognised as equally significant. The bossiness, the occasional bully-boy tactics, the shouting are all expressions of a step-parent's fight against his or her subordinated rank. It is a refusal to come second. Once again, such a refusal can be ugly to witness.

In asking a stepchild to obey, a step-parent has made him- or herself dependent on their stepchild's reaction. If obedience follows, this is taken as a mark of respect. Disobedience on the other hand cannot be tolerated, as it is read as belittling a figure who wants to be revered. Although the domineering step-parent is determined to show that they are in control, they are in fact being controlled by their stepchildren's perception of their role in the family. Under no circumstances should a step-parent ever slide into being so enslaved to the reactions of their stepchildren. A sensible adult does not look to his or her stepchildren for endorsement. Validation comes from our partner.

Every step-parent who is tempted to assert their authority would do well to remember that this a gross misunderstanding of our role. It is time to hang up those bossy boots, find a comfy arm-chair and read a favourite magazine.

Supercalifragilisticexpialidocious Step-parent Syndrome

Women in particular easily fall pray to the ambition to be über-mum. The problem is when they want to be super-mummy to somebody else's children, who already have their own mummy, wherever she may be.

As this oh-so-lovely stepmother whizzes about decked out in her gingham pinny and touching smiles, she is propelled onwards and upwards by the thought that she is doing a great job. A better job in fact than her stepchildren's own mother. The cookies may be delicious and the house wonderfully clean, but the motivation is suspicious. This is someone who wants to win the mothering crown. Without quite realising what is going on, she gets involved in a unfortunate contest which she can of course never win.

Biological parenthood cannot be mimicked. As mentioned earlier, wanting to be a mother to your stepchildren only complicates mat-ters. Mothers are loved in a specific way whereas we may not be loved at all. On the other hand, over time most stepchildren do come to value and love a stable, detached step-parent who is a source of security and affection. But it is a different relationship.

Getting to grips with the nature of our role means accepting the gulf that separates biological from step-parenthood. Learn to think of yourself not as super-mum but as someone who is simply there to help out.

Summary of a step-parent's role

Here are the three key points that define our role:

- Although we are part of the team that shapes our

stepfamily function, we accept that our stepchildren need us less than they need our partner

- In this regard, we are less significant and less important than our partner. We are therefore happy to come second
- One day we will be valued precisely because we know that our role is not to lead but to support

Practical Exercise

Go back to your Step-parenting Record. Open up a new, blank page, pencil at the ready. Think back over the recent months and locate an episode that left you feeling frustrated. Try to break down what went on here by asking yourself whether your behaviour could be fitted into any of the five models of bad step-parenting listed above. Then:

1. Recognise that your vulnerabilities shape the nature of your own agenda
2. Resolve to do better. Concentrate this resolve into a simple phrase that will help to keep you on the straight and narrow, e.g. 'I must not criticise Dave'; 'I must not shout at my stepson'
3. You can also come up with your own affirmation that is a proud, inspiring statement of your position, e.g. 'I am strong enough to stop trying to be liked'

Getting It Across

Once we have mastered the basics of what it is to be a step-parent, we must capitalise on this new-found knowledge by communicating our confidence directly to our stepchildren. Whenever tension begins to grow, nip it in the bud by addressing their fears head-on.

Developing a sense of when to say it like it is can be of enormous benefit. We have a capacity to understand what's going on which a child does not, and sharing that understanding is often a good policy. Here are a few obvious examples of such communication:

- 'Look, it is strange having me around, I know that. But it's strange for me as well'
- 'Of course you miss your dad. He's a special person. He'll always be your dad. I'm only here because I love your mum. But I think you're pretty cool too'
- 'Hey, why the sulking just because I asked you to brush your teeth? Daddy wants you to hang on to your teeth, and so do I for that matter!'
- 'If your mother says you can take the car, fine. I'm not going to interfere'
- 'I know you'd rather that Daddy read your bedtime story, but he's not here. Would you like me to read you one instead?'

Convincing your stepchildren that you are not out to block access to their parent and that you do in fact want the best for them is a never-ending process. Sometimes we can spell this out in black and white; other times we can be more subtle, using indirect methods to make it plain that we are content to hang back. Like much of step-parenting, it is a good habit that gets easier with practice.

Adoption

Sometimes, a step-parent may wish to formally adopt his or her stepchildren.[5] In one sense adoption represents freedom to parent, to be absolved from some of the internal restrictions that limit a step-parent's function as described above. Following adoption, a former step-parent has not only legal authority over a former stepchild, but also greater job security. And this must be part of its attraction.

In the right circumstances, adoption is a powerful way of demonstrating commitment to a stepchild. It can also 'normalise' a non-traditional situation, and as we know this desire to conform to the 'ideal type' of a first marriage with kids is a strong current in most stepfamilies.

Adoption of stepchildren is a popular move in the USA, much more popular than in Britain, Australia or Canada. This is undoubtedly due to the fact that step-parents have few legal rights over their stepchildren unless they formally adopt them (see Appendix). Since 1987 the number of adoptions in the States annually has remained fairly constant, ranging from 118,000 to 127,000. The last year in which the National Center for State Courts assimilated country-wide figures was 1992, and over this twelve-month period step-parent adoptions accounted for 42 per cent of the total. In 2001, the British courts made 4,452 adoption orders. Of these 1,333 were made to step-parents, which is 30 per cent of the total. Interestingly, the adoption rate has fallen off dramatically in Australia. Compare the figures for 1971–2, when there were 10,000 adoptions, to the most recent figures for 2000–1, which numbered only 514. It is an extraordinary contrast.

The courts take great care when it comes to making an adoption order. Before such an order is made, the court must be absolutely satisfied that it is in the best interests of the child. The received wisdom here is that if an absent biological parent still plays a role, however minor, in his or her child's life, then adoption is not a suitable course as it is deemed to interfere with that child's relationship with their natural parent.

Our legal systems are reluctant to sideline a living natural parent who may not be that involved now but could theoretically become involved some time in the future, because a living but absent biological parent is heavily disadvantaged once his or her child has been adopted by someone else. Contact is usually severed, although increasingly courts favour 'open adoptions', whereby an absent bioparent is permitted to stay in touch with their offspring following adoption. However, all post-adoption contact is regulated by the specific terms of the order made in that case. Unless such a provision is included, an absent biological parent has no right of access to his or her child following adoption.

Clearly adoption is less controversial if a natural parent has died. The enormity of adoption is however still recognised by the raft of legislation that defines the support services contingent upon the process. In America, Australia, Canada and Britain, adoption agencies are obliged to carry out assessments subsequent to adoption. It is after all a monumental change in a child's life.

The Stable Step-parent

Defining an appropriate role for the step-parent has been acknowledged time and again as the core difficulty of stepfamily life. The psychologist Margaret Crosbie-Burnett, one of the leading experts in this field, pinpoints ambiguity over boundaries as one of the main causes of stepfamily conflict.[6] The aim of the second cornerstone is to resolve these ambiguities and ultimately to know what to expect of ourselves as step-parents. Having a better sense of the limited nature of our involvement boosts confidence. We are in control now because we know when to hang back and can accept that to a large degree we come second.

On this new, stable footing, a step-parent can relax. We are not trying to prove anything or embody some phoney ideal. We're just being ourselves, one half of a couple, helping our partner deal with the kids. Armed with this perspective a step-parent is 'more likely to approach the inevitable difficulties with positive, problem-solving strategies'.[7]

Certainty is what it's all about. This is echoed by Visher and Visher, 'The children almost always find relief as soon as step-parents become more certain in their relationship with each other and in their dealings with their stepchildren.'[8] This sentence encapsulates the first and second cornerstones, the building blocks for a successful stepfamily.

8

Realistic Expectations

In the preceding chapters, the experience of the step-parent has been in the spotlight. Getting to grips with your step-parenting identity, looking for support from the right person and learning about the limits of your role underpin the first and second cornerstones. Now in preparation for the third cornerstone, the focus shifts away from the step-parent and on to the stepchildren.

What your stepchildren bring into your stepfamily in terms of assumptions, prejudice and pain has direct impact. As a step-parent you know this already; more than likely, it's you who's in the firing line.

Being on the receiving end of aggression, outright dislike, anger and even hatred eats into our capacity to be objective. Instead of feeling sympathy, we feel attacked. We lose interest in their problems because it is these same problems that are making our lives a misery. In these circumstances, a step-parent retreats into his or her own shell, no longer wanting to understand what is actually going on for anyone else. And this can quickly tip over into self-absorption.

But dwelling on just how tough things are for you personally is not going to improve relations between you and your step-children. It amounts to opting out of the domestic matrix that is your stepfamily. Instead of fostering a victim mentality, it's important to believe that you can rejoin the gang. Recapturing your ability to be rational is an essential part of this process.

The Split Personality of a Step-parent

When a step-parent feels under attack, it's easy to forget that there are two sides to every story. Our own experience takes over, blotting out our ability to see the whole. Flailing about in a pit of negative emotions, the struggling step-parent may not want to think about the other stepfamily members, where they are coming from and what they are going through. Being miserable is at odds with making such an effort.

And yet making an effort is, as we know, at the heart of good step-parenting. You and your stepchildren are only bound together by what one psychologist has termed 'the slender thread of remarriage'.[1] The step relationship requires constant vigilance, care and above all commitment. In other words, pulling yourself out of that pit of negativity and forcing yourself to see what's actually going on all around you is imperative.

The awkwardness of the step dynamic can push us into a spate of childish reactions, sulks, tantrums, jealousy. This is of course one of the key frustrations of being a step-parent: we don't want to feel like an irrational child. Asserting your ability to be rational puts you back in the driving seat.

At any given moment, your emotions should be balanced by your clinical observations of your stepfamily; at no time should one side outweigh the other. Your feelings should not be dominant. By the same token, the feelings of others do not eclipse the relevance of how you feel.

Being simultaneously both objective and subjective is in fact a skill that we all practise in everyday life. Sometimes this double-think breaks down which can spell disaster: road rage is an example of childish feelings outweighing reason. Luckily most of us manage to avoid such imbalance.

Out in the world, we are all used to being two people at once, hiding emotional turbulence behind the mask of the civilised adult. Translating double-think into the home, however, can be a difficult business. We want to switch off at home, relax and not have to mentally tiptoe around. In short, we are loathe to use our critical faculties because this smacks of work.

But zoning out is a dangerous course of action for a step-parent. If we abandon the invisible scales and give in to our impulses, there is nothing to regulate the extreme emotions that can upset our equilibrium. In short, step-parents function best as split personalities.

Personally, I have an almost visual image of my better step-mothering self. The sensible stepmother watches on as I slide into loneliness, rejection or anger. It is she who points out that my husband is right there, offering me love and reassurance, if only I could see it.

Your Part in Their Drama

Being objective about the individuals in your stepfamily is a great way of minimising anguish. So much of the situation that you now find yourself in has nothing to do with you. The incoming step-parent is only the latest addition to a line-up that has been in existence for years. And yet this obvious truth is easily forgotten once you've been absorbed into their drama.

Step-parents are quickly duped into believing that they are at the very epicentre of the turmoil. We may come to believe that we are the cause of the trouble. We blame ourselves and at the same time feel angry because we have done nothing wrong.

Getting a raw deal is an unpleasant experience. We all like to be treated with fairness. A citizen is innocent until proven guilty – unless of course that citizen happens to have stepchildren. In these circumstances, there is no such thing as a fair trial.

Without being present or being able to defend yourself in any way, sentence has been passed. The process is swift. Your stepchildren have made up their minds. Being on the receiving end of such arbitrary treatment is enough to make anyone feel aggrieved.

To the new step-parent, this sense of injustice feeds into all the other difficult emotions that go with the territory such as low self-esteem, depression, anger and guilt. Soon one side of the scales is outweighing the other. Instead of being a split personality, there is only one viewpoint. The better step-parenting self doesn't get a look-in.

Take the following case of a stepmother who focused on a single issue and fell into a spiral of angry self-pity as a result. Jody's two teenage stepchildren would visit for the day but were always keen to get back to their mum.

> Sometimes it would be OK with James and Deals. But it was always there, you know, the rejection of us and of our home. I mean, why was it such a big deal where they got their kip? It would've saved everyone so much driving if they'd only agreed to stay. As it was we were locked up in the car for hours on these contact days, ferrying them to and fro.
>
> It was literally the first thing I'd think looking at them: Why won't you just stay the night? What's so wrong with us? Of course they'd been quite happy to stay before I moved in with their father. So that was it – I had to take it personally. And then I couldn't shake it off . . . It ruined my relationship with them for ages.

Over time, however, Jody came to realise that there was more to this than met the eye. She'd assumed that her stepchildren, being

16 and 14, were free agents. What she'd left out of the equation was their mother and her feelings. To stay the night at their dad's had become somehow off-limits.

> Something clicked, slowly, not overnight, but slowly I knew that these kids had no choice. It wasn't so much them rejecting me as their mother rejecting me and my husband. It happens all the time, I know. But it isn't right.
>
> That was it. Once I felt sorry for them I sort of stopped feeling sorry for myself. Instead of thinking, Poor little me, I felt, Poor them, those poor kids. And it was surprising really what a difference that made. Somehow the tension went out of the visits after that. I stopped dreading the contact. We get along fine now. They don't stay the night ever but that's natural enough in teenagers. They want to get back to their own base.

This is a great example of someone who has managed to detach and see more than her own painful reactions. Although nothing in this woman's situation had changed, she felt radically different about what she had to deal with. Her better step-parenting self won through, holding up a mirror to reflect the totality of the situation. And after that her life as a stepmother improved. She took the pressure off herself and in doing so took the tension out of their dynamic.

Loaded Dice

Trapped in the crossfire of another couple's failed marriage or plunged into the midst of another family's grief following bereavement, a step-parent is instantly out of his or her depth. The dice are loaded against us from the start. A sharp sense of injustice takes hold and before we know it a constant cry of 'It's not fair!' is circling round and round our minds.

Reactions to a step-parent are largely predetermined. Although you think your character is what swings people for or against, your character has little to do with how you will be treated as a step-parent. What's relevant here is simply the gap you're filling.

The step-parent who is geared up to receive less than nothing from the stepchildren is doing him- or herself the most enormous favour. Their behaviour may seem off-kilter, unwarranted or plain awful. Instead of asking yourself whether you deserve to be treated in this way, shrug your shoulders and take yourself out of the equation. They have their pain and this is how it's being expressed.

- Accept that becoming a step-parent means enduring the fall-out from the breakdown of your partner's previous relationship. The extent of this fall-out was determined at the time of the breakdown
- How your stepchildren cope with your appearance on the scene reflects the level of post-breakdown fall-out, whether this was caused by death or divorce
- Their reaction to you is largely fixed before they've even met you. Step-parents must not rail against their fate. Bite the bullet and accept that the dice are loaded
- Pull yourself up short every time you feel like muttering, 'It's not fair.' Remind yourself that this kind of thinking is only going to hold you back
- Instead of feeling like a victim, take control. Let your better step-parenting self bring the big picture into focus
- Remember that although things may be tough for you they are also tough for your stepchildren. They have their pain and you are a useful peg on which to hang their troubles
- It is however vital that you are treated with basic levels of respect and courtesy. Together both of you should enforce this policy of respect. As set out in the first cornerstone,

the stepchildren must understand from their own mother
or father that they cannot be rude to you

Your stepchildren respond to you not because of what you're
like as a person but simply because of the space you occupy in
their lives. Anybody stepping into the vacancy would be subjected to the same thumbs-down.

The trauma of acquiring a step-parent can remain fresh for
decades. This was certainly true in the following case history, in
which a stepdaughter recalls events that occurred over thirty
years ago:

> I was fifteen when my dad married Tabitha and I could not have
> felt more betrayed. Because I was living with my father, just the
> two of us, it was a kind of perfect life for me at that time. My
> mother was not around and so Daddy and I, we had these perfect
> times that seemed so complete to me.
>
> But obviously he was a man with his own needs and he wanted
> a mate and so he found one. I was horrified because I thought we
> were fine as we were. Although I was fifteen, part of me just could
> not understand why he needed her when he had me. And she was
> so dreary, and I was so fun . . . none of it made sense to my
> immature mind. But I have to say that as a couple they were
> happy for years and years, although I could never ever understand
> why.

In the above account, the stepmother's personality remains a
blank. Her character was largely irrelevant; it was what she rep-
resented that was of enormous significance. Her arrival signalled
the end of an era. The wicked stepmother had got in the way.

This is frequently the lot of the step-parent. We are obstacles
that block the channels between child and parent, between ex-
wife and ex-husband. By definition, we get in the way of what
others would like to believe. Being a step-parent often means

being the scapegoat. If only you hadn't come along, everything would be fine. Why is my dad with hideous you anyway? He should be back with us, in our house! My mum loves my dad more than she loves you! I never wanted a stepfather! Just leave us alone! Belonging in the present, the new partner essentially gets in the way of the past. And this can be painful for everyone.

What the Step-parent Represents

All children are held in the grip of two conflicting but subconscious desires. They want their mummy and daddy to be together but they also want to push them apart so that they have the lion's share of an isolated parent's attention. These tensions exist in all intact families. However, when an original unit has come undone these desires can take on alarming new dimensions.

Once the stable structure of a married couple has broken down, a child openly craves his or her parents to be reunited. This craving is agonising, and also confusing as it is offset by a weird awareness that they now have what they subliminally always wanted, which was the monopoly of their mother or father. After a breakdown, a child is free to fantasise about being the absolute focus of a parent's love.

The heartbreak of divorce or the tragedy of bereavement is an enormous trauma for all concerned. The loss, the fluid grief that continues for years, is a harsh legacy to cope with, regardless of age. In the wreckage, a child clings to whichever parent happens to be at hand. The parent's guilt about causing such suffering to their offspring intensifies the dynamic. The child is indeed the focus, so a fantasy has been realised and this affords some small compensation to the younger generation.

Introduce a step-parent and that compensation instantly vanishes. A child no longer has the monopoly of a protector's attention. Now that Mummy or Daddy has a new partner, the only possible good thing that resulted from their divorce has gone too. There is nothing worse than sharing a parent with a stranger.

The arrival of a step-parent represents a double blow for the children. The dream of their mother and father being reunited comes under massive strain. Just by being there, a step-parent is depriving this reunion fantasy of vital oxygen. And then your relationship with their parent is depriving them of their exclusive monopoly of Mum or Dad, as this stepdaughter explained to me:

> When we were little, we'd wake up and scamper into Mum's room and climb into bed. That was always how we started the day unless my stepfather was around. He had to go away a lot on business, and so he often wasn't around. But when he was at home, their bedroom was off-limits.
>
> The door was kept locked. Of course when Mum was alone, the door would be open. I do remember this strong sense of there being this marriage, their marriage, and then there were us children, who were kept separate. And that big divide always remained. We never just mucked about together as one family.

As this woman's experience makes clear, a step-parent can represent the end of hope. In the lives of the stepchildren, you are a walking reminder that their dreams can never be fulfilled. And that unfortunately is enough to tip many a stepchild into furious resentment.

Sex and the Green-Eyed Monster

Sex causes a lot of problems for even the youngest children. A buried awareness of sex is knitted into the fabric of early childhood. There comes an age when this translates into open knowledge. And then the fireworks really begin. The truth dawns that their parent is doing something with you that is way outside a child's domain.

Just as a step-parent will always be an outsider in terms of blood lines, a child remains outside the private world of adult sexuality. And if your stepchildren are of primary-school age or above, they will be aware of and frustrated by this strange power that you have over their mum or dad. By this logic, you have an unfair advantage.

I found this out with one of my stepdaughters. Our stepfamily had been up and running for about three years when things suddenly took a turn for the worse. Literally overnight, this little girl could neither look at nor speak to me. The weekend was a disaster and so was the following one. It was winter and a depressingly bleak time. Nothing improved over the next month. She avoided my gaze, and ignored any attempts at conversation. She simply did not want to know.

Finally, I asked my other stepdaughter what was up, which was obviously something I should have done long before. 'Oh, her friend told her about the facts of life when we were staying with them at new year. She doesn't like the sound of it . . .' On one hand, I was relieved that such a solid reason lay behind her wall of silence, but on the other hand, I was worried that this was causing her quite so much trouble. Dad pitched in, dispensing crude British humour left, right and centre. Benny Hill would've approved: every other word was 'knickers'. The strategy worked, and she started to laugh again.

Getting to grips with the notion of sex prompts many a stepchild to re-evaluate how they fit into their stepfamily. Although confident with their own parent, they are less confident around the couple that the parent now belongs to. The sense that they are somehow less relevant takes hold. I was told of one stepdaughter who clearly felt superfluous once her stepfather had moved in. He elaborated:

Just after I moved in with her mum, my thirteen-year-old step-daughter revealed that she was desperate to go to boarding school. Her mum thought it was a joke at first, but then it got to a point when she was too insistent for us to laugh it off any more. But it was strange because Lily wasn't one of those kids who's comfortable with institutions like school or Brownies or whatever. She's a bit of a free spirit, in her way rather anti-establishment. So we had no idea where this was coming from.

Then there was this one time where she made some jibe, I can't remember exactly what, but along the lines of us being so happy together, and suddenly it clicked. Lily thought that we didn't want her around. Not wanting to be pushed out, she wanted to take herself out, to leave home.

Being proud, Lily wanted to be in charge, to get there first if you like. Her mum had to provide a hell of a lot of reassurance before she calmed down.

Unavoidably, your stepchildren are on some level threatened by your sex life. A child's own jealousy is supplemented by a painful awareness that their parent is having sex with the wrong person. And where does this leave their absent mother or father? Unless the absent parent has also found someone new, the fear gels in a child's heart that their absent parent is suffering. This reinforces their desire to protect the mother or father whose position you now occupy, which of course intensifies their hostility towards you.

Loyalty to an Absent Parent

In fantasising that their parents should be back together, stepchildren subscribe to a belief system which stops them from liking you. The idea of liking this person who is getting in the way of their absent parent's happiness creates enormous conflict. If they like you, they are betraying their mum or dad. In this situation there is no choice: a step-parent is hated not out of choice but out of loyalty.

Children are at the mercy of powerful emotions which they do not understand and cannot regulate. My stepdaughters are no exception to the rule. As far as they were concerned, I had a lot to answer for. Their father belonged with their mother, and this unshakeable belief expressed itself in a wall of hostility. I remember one instance particularly vividly. Eighteen months into my life as a stepmother, we planned a holiday which both my stepdaughters were looking forward to enormously. Checking in at the hotel, we decided that I was to sleep in one room with our baby, and that my husband was to share the other room with his girls.

After unpacking, I knocked on their door. As I walked inside, one of the girls took one look at me and let rip, shrieking that this was their room, that they didn't want me here, claiming that Daddy had promised that I wouldn't be allowed in their room. Horrified, I retreated. Was her claim true? Had there been some kind of agreement about this between herself and her dad? The whole thing shook me to the core.

The desperate craving to have Daddy all to herself led my stepdaughter to scale new heights of aggression. When she'd calmed down, her father took her to one side and explained that she had to apologise, which she duly did. Ironically, six years later she can only dimly recall this showdown, whereas I can still replay the incident in all its Technicolor glory.

This episode was early on in my life as a stepmother, so there was only one way of responding to this showdown, which was to feel personally rejected. My mind reeling, I wondered how on earth we would get through this. I just wanted out, to run away and begin a new life without stepchildren. Nowadays my defences are in position:

- I accept that as a step-parent I am going to be the scapegoat
- These explosions can be tolerated because they are not

personal. To my stepchildren, I am a punchbag that comes in useful when the pain of their past gets too much

- I can choose how to respond to their hostility, which means exerting a great deal of self-control and keeping cool. When lacking the strength to cope and feeling vulnerable, I either take time out or turn to my partner to rebuild my defences
- Nevertheless it is not acceptable for my stepchildren to believe that their hostility has no consequences. They must adhere to house rules; when explosions happen, these should be followed sometimes with talk but always with apologies
- I know what I can provide and what I am responsible for
- I also know that I am *not* responsible for their loss, despite what they believe. However, my stepchildren *are* entitled to their beliefs, no matter how far-fetched
- What they choose to believe about me is really an expression of their suffering and has nothing to do with me, even when directed at me personally
- One day my stepchildren will appreciate that I want the best for them and have worked hard for their benefit over the years

Getting Your Expectations into Shape

Acquiring stepchildren is a universally acknowledged challenge. Yet the challenge that we step-parents represent to children is of a far greater magnitude. And, as the adult generation, we have the luxury of retreating into our grown-up lives. Unlike our stepchildren, we have moved on from a world which is all about Mum and Dad.

Fury at what has been taken away and fear that you will deprive them of the little that they have left are all part of a stepchild's lot. As the newcomer, you will inevitably be harassed by issues that still provoke and pain a stepchild.

And yet as weeks become months and months turn into years, you can establish a positive relationship which will help to keep their demons at bay. It isn't easy to behave well when you are scorned. Let your better step-parenting self intervene when you feel at the end of your tether. Remember to switch focus away from yourself and on to the troubles that oppress your step-children, enabling you to keep control instead of snapping.

9

The Third Cornerstone:
Keep Rejection at Arm's Length

Coping with antagonistic stepchildren is an effort of will. It is a Herculean task stopping yourself from retaliating in kind. Even though we may want to snap back, we know in our heart of hearts that such retaliation is only going to make things worse. The question that faces every step-parent is: how can you remain calm when the assault begins?

Keeping calm is at the heart of good step-parenting. If you have organised a treat for a stepchild who then refuses to get in the car, what do you do? Do you stamp and shout and let your stepchild see that he or she has really pressed your buttons? Or can you digest this bitter disappointment without letting rip?

This is where life gets particularly hard for the step-parent. 'There are so many moving parts to a stepfamily, that it is open to more conflicts than the usual [intact] family.'[1] Anyone let down in this way would have every right to be cross. However, the harsh reality is that it is always better to swallow your fury and put on a brave face. In essence, what this means is relinquishing your right to stand up for yourself.

Clearly this goes against the grain, because we are conditioned to stand up for ourselves from an early age. Society places a high premium on being able to defend your turf. In deciding to treat your stepchild to a great day out, you are investing part of yourself in that choice. When the stepchild declines to co-operate and refuses to get in the car, it can seem like a rejection not only of the plan but of you personally. You are wounded on a deep level.

Coping with these hurt feelings is the crux of the matter. Some fortunate step-parents are so well-balanced that they never slide into a wounded state. Most of us however are vulnerable to the barbs of aggressive stepchildren, whether we are pushed towards anger or tears, anxiety or paranoia.

These negative emotions destroy our mental well-being, but maintaining our equilibrium is essential for the step-parent. Although natural parents are just as likely to be infuriated by their offspring, both parent and child are secure in the uncondi-tional love that binds them together. This creates a bedrock of trust which cushions them against the harmful effects of a scream-ing match. The truth is that children actively want to forgive their parents. However, where a step-parent is concerned the reverse is true. Stepchildren do not want to forgive someone who has com-plicated their lives.

The initial trauma was their parents' break-up. Getting a step-parent is collateral damage.

Many stepchildren carry this sense of grievance into adulthood: if only the cursed step-parent wasn't on the scene, everything in the garden would be rosy. This kind of unrealistic thinking is infu-riating. It is like living in parallel worlds: the one where you and your partner dwell and the one that your stepchildren inhabit. And of course, being parallel, the two can never meet.

Allowing your stepchildren to believe what they like about you is one of the very hardest lessons that we have to learn. As discussed in the previous chapter, when you become a step-parent your stepchildren have already written many of your lines for you. Because they only breathe in the atmosphere of their universe, they want you to conform to their version of reality. Part of them is desperately urging you to fill the wicked stepmother/cruel stepfather mould.

So are we going to live up to their worst nightmares, confirming all their prejudices along the way? Are we going to lose our temper? Stepchildren almost will us into being the step-parent of their imagination, seizing on moments when we have done them wrong and magnifying these tenfold.

A step-parent can either give in to negativity or decide to rise to the challenge. In refusing to live up to their worst imaginings, you are committing yourself to a hard road. You are undertaking a pledge to exercise supreme self-control during the most testing of times. It is a promise to be the best person you possibly can be; to stay in your universe, where you know you are good, and not slip into their world of fictionalised evil.

Children are reared on a black-and-white understanding of good and bad. The fairy-tale diet of malevolent stepmothers distorts perception from an early age. (Stepfathers don't get a good press either, from Hamlet's loathing of Claudius to the present-day preoccupations with abuse.) There are thus two layers of bias against the step-parent: resistance born out of personal experience is overlaid with the general consensus that step-parents spell trouble. Given this toxic combination, it is hardly surprising that stepchildren choose to stay in their universe where they know what is what: mums and dads are great but step-parents are not.

Keeping rejection at arm's length is the only chance that a step-parent has to disprove all those negative assumptions. Rise to the occasion and do not react, even when pushed to the limits. This is a skill that must be learned and fine-tuned and endlessly applied.

Arbitration at Home

It would be fantastic if there was a universal method of safe-guarding a step-parent's sanity. We can all feel a little crazy when subjected to a long roll-call of ambivalent treatment. One of my stepdaughters insists on addressing general questions to her father alone, even though we are both in the room and I could provide an answer just as well.

Over the years this persistent reflex has hurt my feelings big-time. Am I invisible? Why don't I qualify as someone who could answer? Is she cross with me? What have I done wrong? In a trice, the wail 'It's not fair' is bubbling up inside me and the strops begin.

My stepdaughter's habit of addressing only her father is how-ever on one level just that – a habit. I may find it upsetting but that is just my side of the story. After their separation, it was just Dad coping with his kids at weekends. Arguably, this little girl is per-haps still locked in that phase of her life. In one way, she is closing her eyes and remembering a time when I wasn't around. Seen from this perspective, her inability to acknowledge my presence is much more to do with her pain.

There are two distinct types of rejecting behaviour. The first category consists of behaviour that you personally find upset-ting but which may not, to an outside observer, seem rejecting at all. Nobody overhearing my stepdaughter ask, 'Dad, where's the phone?' would think she was having a go at me. Objectively speaking there's nothing to report. The second category includes behaviour that is so plainly intended to provoke that an outside observer would immediately detect its hostility. Direct attacks, confrontations, insults and slights are just some of the openly aggressive tactics that can be thrown at a step-parent. And yet all these antisocial fireworks spring from the same root, which is the inner disturbance of our stepchildren. Recognising the extent of their confusion is a trick discussed in the previous chapter.

Working with this two-tier classification is useful because it sorts out your baggage from your stepchildren's baggage. In the first category, the turmoil produced by a perceived slight is the result of the step-parent's own issues. 'Dad, where's the phone?' is not inflammatory but still used to wind me up because my own baggage got in the way. Some people can weather being ignored better than others. For me, it's a flashpoint for my insecurities.

Of course there are times when your stepchildren are actively hostile towards you, which is the deliberate rejection of the second category. If you go to pick up your stepchildren from school and they groan and protest on seeing you, this is by anyone's standards hurtful. Yet this is so clearly a reflection of their difficulties adjusting that it isn't really to do with you at all. Behaviour in this category springs from your stepchildren's baggage. They focus their complaints on you because of the space that you occupy in their lives.

Learning to distinguish between these two different types of hurt is the prerequisite for keeping rejection at arm's length. Although the net result of both is the same, establishing the origins will present you with the right remedy. You are the judge here, assessing not only your own conduct but the conduct of those around you. Don't be biased in your own favour. It's easy to think that everyone else is to blame. If you're going to get this right, you have to be fair.

Use the flowchart below to track the origin of your malaise.

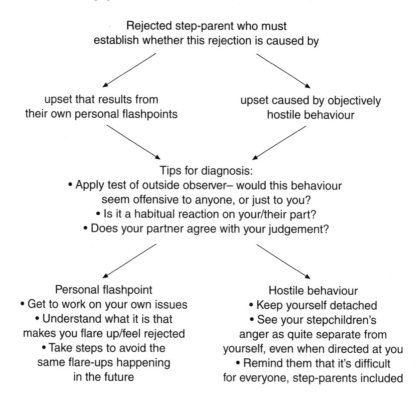

Rejected step-parent who must
establish whether this rejection is caused by

upset that results from
their own personal flashpoints

upset caused by objectively
hostile behaviour

Tips for diagnosis:
• Apply test of outside observer– would this behaviour
seem offensive to anyone, or just to you?
• Is it a habitual reaction on your/their part?
• Does your partner agree with your judgement?

Personal flashpoint
• Get to work on your own issues
• Understand what it is that
makes you flare up/feel rejected
• Take steps to avoid the
same flare-ups happening
in the future

Hostile behaviour
• Keep yourself detached
• See your stepchildren's
anger as quite separate from
yourself, even when directed at you
• Remind them that it's difficult
for everyone, step-parents included

Recognising Your Own Issues

It can take a while to locate the specific problems that derail our equilibrium. We know well enough when we have been thrown off track by our stepchildren; feelings of unhappy exasperation are familiar territory. But actually acknowledging that you yourself are magnifying tensions does not come easily to any of us. And yet we all know that we have our own areas of sensitivity, our own flashpoints which if triggered can cause a situation to explode.

We may not understand why we are so sensitive when it comes to a particular issue. What matters however is the actual recognition of these personal blind spots. Owning up to the less than lovely aspects of our character requires self-discipline. It is not a cosy experience, as this stepmother's account so neatly demonstrates:

I grew up knowing I was right. Whatever it was, I had the answers. On the little details, I outshone everybody else. As a child, I was a know-it-all because I *did* know it all. Sometimes I felt proud, like I was extra clever. Then in my teens, it dawned on me that this talent of mine was pissing everyone off, so I dropped it pretty quick.

Unfortunately, sometime in my thirties I reverted to type. My husband teases me about it all the time but even he gets annoyed. So I try to keep a lid on it but don't always manage. Trouble is, I usually am right, especially about directions.

One day we were in the car, me and my husband and his fifteen-year-old son, Matthew. We were driving out to a paint-ball [event]. I knew the way and told my husband to leave the motorway at whatever junction it was. But Matthew said that he'd been before and it was better to carry on. It was like a red rag to a bull – I just lost it. I screamed and shouted that he didn't know what he was talking about, that I was right, how dare he contradict me and so on. It was humiliating. Afterwards I felt ashamed.

An outside observer witnessing this scene would not have criticised the stepson for offering his opinion as to the best route. Matthew wasn't rude, he just didn't agree with his stepmother's advice. Her own baggage caused her to overreact.

What we think is important in life is strongly connected to our vulnerabilities. We are sensitive about the things that we hold dear to our heart. Take the above example: being right was a critical issue for this woman. Personally, I have always been rather over-sentimental, believing in the importance of communicating affection, because this is exactly what I need – a large amount of affection. If what an individual needs is not met, or if it is frustrated or demeaned, we become vulnerable.

I put myself on the line repeatedly with my stepdaughters, exposing my own vulnerability over and over again until I learned better. Whenever they were staying over, I wanted to kiss them good-night. Often I read them a story and tucked them up in bed but at the final hurdle they would bury their faces in their pillows, protesting that they only liked Mummy's kisses. How many times did I set myself up for a fall of this kind? I lost count. Something in me made me seek out this holy grail of a good-night kiss, which my stepdaughters refused to provide. Eventually I trained myself out of the habit. From then on, I felt fine because I kept my neediness to myself.

Making a conscious decision to master our blind spots requires brute honesty. It's painful to acknowledge that we are at fault. However, if you think of what you will gain by putting your character under the microscope, the process becomes worthwhile. In understanding your own blind spots, you will win your freedom from a damaging cycle of paranoia.

Being paranoid is believing that those around us are out to do us down, which is exactly what happens when we allow our stepchildren to ride roughshod over our sensibilities. Like entering a competition to which only we know the rules, we reveal our weaknesses and expect our stepchildren to notice and respect them. When they fail this secret test, we lose our tempers, feeling hurt and annoyed, sliding into believing that they did it on purpose, when in fact they'd never actually been told the rules of the competition.

To summarise:

- When tempers fray, apply the test of the outside observer. If objective analysis shows that your stepchildren have not behaved anti-socially, then you must turn the spotlight on yourself
- Try to work out why you lost your equilibrium. Remember that being the step-parent often makes us feel insecure because we feel unloved by our stepchildren
- If you detect yourself feeling jealous, focus on the first cornerstone: YOU AND YOUR PARTNER ARE A TEAM. Make sure

you are getting enough reassurance and appreciation from
your partner

- If you feel ignored or taken for granted, remember the
  second cornerstone: KNOW YOUR ROLE. Readjust your
  expectations, learn to take a back seat and accept that you
  will never be as important to your stepchildren as your
  partner is
- If however you detect that your own vulnerabilities
  caused you to lose the plot, then you need to acknowledge
  this source of danger
- Our own painful issues cause pain and create tension, not
  only for ourselves but for those around us. Because we
  want to KEEP REJECTION AT ARM'S LENGTH, we must make an
  effort to contain these areas of over-sensitivity and not let
  them destroy the delicate balance of stepfamily life
- Commit yourself to avoiding a recurrence of the same
  problem in the future

Every step-parent needs a hefty dose of self-awareness as insur-
ance against their own frailties. However, when it's not you but
your stepchildren who have been objectively diagnosed as the
source of tension, it is time to use all your strength to stop their
hurtful behaviour from hitting home. The aim here is to KEEP
REJECTION AT ARM'S LENGTH.

Recognising the Frustration of Your Stepchildren

To your stepchildren, you are primarily an abstract shapeless
step-parent-thing. Your personality may or may not be allowed
a look-in, depending on the extent of their negative assumptions.

Being a step-parent means assuming an identity that is quite separate from yourself. We must learn to exercise our split personality, taking ourselves out of the equation of what is happening around us. When we are all wrapped up in our stepparent cloak, what they are really insulting is the cloak that we're wearing, not the character inside.

Human nature determines that we are all self-absorbed, which tempts us into believing that the behaviour of our stepchildren must have something to do with us and how we behave. We fall into the trap of thinking that their antagonism is a response to things that we have said and done. In general terms, being self-absorbed is not a serious flaw. But if you're a step-parent, being self-absorbed is a disaster. This was a mistake I made over and over again. Finally I learned to accept that my principal role is that of Abstract Stepmother. My actual character plays the understudy, granted an occasional look-in.

Some lucky step-parents have an instinctive understanding of this difference. Such a practical approach has huge rewards, as demonstrated by this stepfather's account:

> When I moved in, Natasha didn't want anything to do with me. It wasn't planned really, my moving in – it just sort of happened without any of us noticing. Except for Natasha; she noticed all right. She was six – it had been just the two of them, her and her mum. In her book, I was one of the Untouchable caste.
>
> I was full of germs, so Natasha said – that was her opinion and so be it. She wouldn't come near me, literally for months. If she accidentally touched me, she'd go and wash her hands! But slowly it turned into a game. I'd stand outside her bedroom door, putting on a silly voice and squealing, 'It's not Germy, it's Oscarpoposcar.' Silly really, but it ended up being our little routine. She didn't mind talking to Oscar, but she wouldn't talk to Germy.

This stepfather was able not only to detach himself from her alienating remarks but also to come up with a strategy that disarmed her disgust. Instead of taking Natasha's scorn lying down, this clever man found a way of establishing a bond between the two of them.

Remaining cool in the face of your stepchildren's turmoil does not condemn you to being passive. Although the importance of the detached mindset cannot be underestimated, you are not there to be abused at will. As long as you are confident that you are not letting any rejecting behaviour get under your skin, you can respond as you think fit.

In the early years, one of my stepdaughters prided herself on being as rude as possible about my clothes. From an early age, she was into personal style and my lack of it was an easy peg on which to hang her ambivalence about me. I've never cared much about fashion and so was impervious to all the insults. Although I didn't mind about what she was actually saying, it didn't seem responsible to let her get away with being quite so rude. This exchange was a defining moment in the development of our relationship, as if she suddenly realised that there was an actual woman inhabiting the ghoul-figure that was now living with her father.

Respect is a vital component in the nexus between step-parent and stepchild. In standing up for yourself, you are demonstrating that you are not an abstract step-parent-thing but a person to be reckoned with. In being rude to you, or rejecting the things that you do or say, your stepchildren are subconsciously willing you to hand in your resignation.

Letting them get their frustrations out without getting frustrated yourself short-circuits their aggravation and also earns you Brownie points. In showing them that you can handle whatever they throw at you, you earn their respect. By not getting wound up, you are indicating that this adult is here to stay.

There comes a time when their protests should ease off. You can help your stepchildren towards that time by keeping a firm grip on your inner calm. Let them wail and howl and then watch as they pass through the eye of the storm.

To summarise:

- If the stepchildren are venting their fury and being objectively hostile, your self-defence mechanisms should slot into place
- Detach yourself from what is essentially their baggage
- Remember that, even when directed at you personally, this behaviour has nothing to do with you. It is targeted at you because of the space that you occupy in the lives of your stepchildren
- This means that you must make every effort to become the observer. Imagine that these youngsters are unrelated to either you or your partner, but are simply visitors. You wouldn't take it personally if a stranger was rude, you'd just think it was their problem
- You can see hostile behaviour for what it is: expressions of their own anger at what has happened to them and what they have been deprived of
- Because you are not upset, you do not join the fray. Your stepchildren want to upset you; in keeping calm you are defeating their purpose, which raises the possibility that they will settle down
- You can pitch in with whatever contribution you think appropriate, provided that you are composed. You are proving to them that you are a force to be reckoned with and that they cannot intimidate you, thus earning their grudging respect
- Reason with your stepchildren. Put the other side of the story. Explain that it's difficult for all of you to adjust to new circumstances. Make them face up to the consequences of their antisocial behaviour
- If you are able, assert your commitment to your

stepchildren by telling them that no matter what they say or feel about you, come hell or high water you care about them

- In standing firm you are helping them come to terms with the unity of their stepfamily

Practical Exercise

Go back to your Step-parenting Record, pen in hand. Conjure up three specific incidents, when you have felt valued or rewarded by your stepchildren. Get into the habit of recalling these good times when you are down – it isn't all bad!

It is possible to stand back from rejection provided that it does not feed into our personal weaknesses. But there are times when both parties are contributing to the tension. It's not just the step-parent, or the wrathful stepchildren, but a combination of the two. And this is when the fireworks really begin.

When Both Parties Are at Fault

Being in a state ourselves makes it pretty difficult to think about anything apart from our own fragile condition. The motivation behind the assault and what prompted our stepchildren to have a go loses relevance once we are upset. And yet good step-parenting is about forcing yourself to make the effort even when you don't feel like it. You cannot let your anger get in the way of dispute resolution.

So the referee is pointing his finger at both parties: the step-children have been visibly hurtful but the step-parent has overreacted. Each feels wronged by the actions of the other. The step-parent displays his or her fury at being provoked, blaming the stepchildren, who in turn resent being blamed by someone they didn't want in their lives in the first place. There are no winners here. The anger rebounds and intensifies.

Meltdowns of this kind are traumatic for all concerned. The bioparent often feels caught between the warring factions as each side tries to enlist his or her support.

We experienced this high level of conflict for quite a while over one particular issue: the acceptability of my cooking. I have to be honest here, I am not the greatest chef in the world. I was the family laughing stock, the butt of a million jokes, and thus became ridiculously sensitive about my lack of skill in the kitchen. However I've been making edible meals for well over a decade, before my stepdaughters came into my life. And yet the paranoia remains, which means that I am continually anxious about how a meal is going to be received.

Right from the beginning, my stepdaughters used food as a way of rejecting their stepmother. I would produce shepherd's pie, spaghetti or whatever, but they claimed that their mum made it differently and they wouldn't eat, so I would go into a decline. They got me where it hurt.

Pretty quickly stepfamily mealtimes became extremely fraught. Before we even sat down, my tension levels were rocketing as I anticipated rejection. Of course in their terms, they were express-ing loyalty to their mum by not eating what their stepmother had prepared. But I wasn't interested in all that because I was so damned furious. I felt powerless, resentful and victimised.

The solution was so simple, afterwards we wondered why we hadn't thought of it before. My husband took over the cook-ing. He could only make one dish – macaroni cheese – but that didn't seem to matter. Miraculously, the girls would eat his food. And I got a break not only from the stove but from my own paranoia.

If a situation is going badly wrong on a regular basis, you and your partner have to make the time to focus on how you can do better. Here are some helpful pointers:

- Take personal responsibility for trying to work out what exactly is upsetting you
- If your partner hasn't already realised that you're experiencing difficulties, make this clear to him or her and ask for some support. Take comfort in the strength of your partnership
- Accept that your partner is much more likely to be able to understand both sides of the story as he/she loves both you and his/her children. Listen to your partner's version of events, and do not shout down any criticisms of your behaviour
- Remember that step-parents hate admitting that they've got it wrong as they see this as an admission that they are mucking up the job generally
- It's OK to confess that you handled something badly. Your partner should provide you with a backdrop of reassurance which makes owning up to overreactions possible
- The two of you are responsible for preventing the same disaster from occurring again in the future. If your stepchildren are of an age when they can share in this responsibility, then involve them in the process too

Hitting Rock Bottom

The potential for rejection is built into every stepfamily. As a result of not being wanted to the same degree as the bioparent, a step-parent can slide into thinking that he or she is not wanted at all. This easily blurs into hurt feelings, which is why it's so important to KEEP REJECTION AT ARM'S LENGTH. There are times, however, when we fail spectacularly at this task. In these dark hours when rejection hits home you need to have access to a rescue plan.

It takes an enormous amount of determined concentration to

do our job well. We are undergoing an ordeal to which everyone else is oblivious. And occasionally we simply run out of strength, exhausted by the battle to keep marching on despite other people's scorn. At times like this we are drained of all energy. We cannot get up and carry on because we've hit rock bottom. All we want to do is sink into ourselves.

Emotional exhaustion cannot be ignored. It leaves us empty, gutted by what we have experienced. Hopefully a collapse on this scale does not happen too often but when it does, soldiering on is not an option; an exhausted, vulnerable step-parent will only make a mess of things, flaring up, fighting back, losing control and causing trouble.

In the circumstances it's better to admit temporary defeat. Give yourself a break from being a step-parent. Take time out until you feel restored. Don't be a martyr, be sensible. Coping means recognising the need for personal down-time. Doing a little of whatever it is that we find relaxing is an essential pick-me-up when the going gets tough.

My husband got pretty good at recognising when I hit rock bottom, better in fact than me. I'd be getting increasingly hot under the collar without quite seeing that I was at my wit's end. A few times, he presented me with my wellington boots and urged me to get gardening. As soon as I was outside, madly digging and weeding and clipping, calm was restored.

Far from being self-indulgent, therapeutic activities perform a vital function. Whatever it is – gardening, train-spotting, a massage, a game of darts – we all benefit from being allowed to enjoy ourselves. It's good for our self-esteem and therefore good for those around us.

10
The Ex Factor

By definition, our lives as step-parents can only begin because someone else has dropped out of the picture. The space that we now occupy was once filled by a different person, who may be hovering at the edge or shouting from the sidelines, or have left this life altogether. Whether alive or dead, this person holds the title of our partner's previous partner and mother or father of our stepchildren. The ex is a monumental presence in our lives.

If your partner has been bereaved, the memory of the departed spouse remains vivid and the pain of loss lingers on. If the ex is still around, it's easy to feel the rivalry. Negotiating this sense that we are stepping into someone else's shoes is difficult for all of us.

We are shut out from the past that our partner shared with this person. No matter what they tell us, our partners can never convey the totality of their existence as a couple. And through your stepchildren the reality of their past continues, tying your partner both to that era and to the personality of the ex.

The Legacy of the Ex

It is your counterpart who defined the nature of the space that you now occupy. Their role as biological creator cannot be challenged.

The love that a child has for his or her parents is pretty much indestructible, and this is partly why we have such trouble coping with the legacy of the ex. They have beaten us before the race has even begun: our stepchildren will always love the ex more than they love us, which is why it is so important not to compete.

Many of us nurse uncharitable feelings towards our predecessors. We might wish to close our eyes to the existence of the ex, but this is one thing that we cannot do. For the absent parent of your stepchildren continues to be involved in your stepfamily. This involvement can be physical, when an ex is living round the corner and dropping off the kids, or metaphysical in the case of a deceased parent whose memory lives on. To quote the stepson whose mother had died when he was only eleven months old once again:

> I needed to remember my mother but my stepmother needed to forget that she'd ever existed. So right from day one we were in conflict. She was determined to blot out a truth that was an essential part of me. At the end of the day, it's difficult for me to forgive what she did.

Learning to live alongside our partner's previous partner is vital if we are to make a success of the step dynamic. In short, our stepchildren need us to process whatever difficulties we may have in this area. They are much more likely to accept us if we can accept their absent mother or father. Whether this person lives on or has died, there are a few unavoidable truths that every step-parent has to take on board about their biological counterpart:

- We have no control over either the legacy or the personality of our predecessor, and this can make us feel powerless
- Many of us resent the fact that we can do nothing but accept the situation that they created when they were

one half of a couple with the person who is now our partner

- The reality of their past as a couple often makes us uncomfortable and jealous. Our stepchildren are living reminders of their life together
- A step-parent who has not had their own children can feel inadequate for not having experienced biological parenthood
- Every child idealises his/her natural parents. This can grate, especially for full-time step-parents who have taken on all the responsibilities of natural parenthood. We do not want to feel inferior to this person, especially if their practical and emotional contribution is negligible
- We are all too aware of the relationship that binds our stepchildren to their absent mother or father and can feel jealous of it. Coming second in this way can lead to frustration and anger. We resent our automatic subordination
- If you manage to be neutral or even complimentary about your biological counterpart, your stepchildren will respect you for respecting their absent parent. It's not the easiest course to follow, but it's definitely the best

When a Parent Has Died

Coming into a family where your partner has been widowed and your stepchildren have lost a parent is serious stuff. In fact, a bereavement of this magnitude is about as serious as life gets.

Part of the intense difficulty of grieving is trying to work out how to carry on living without the person you have lost. The death of a partner and parent shatters the world that existed for that family. Everything they knew, everything they took for granted has been destroyed. Such grief leaves adults and children alike confused, plagued with doubts and guilt about whether they should even try to carry on or whether they should remain locked up in their loss. They do not know whether recovery is possible, let alone permissible. As someone who is not grief-stricken, the incoming step-parent can facilitate recovery. Unburdened by loss, the new partner brings a much-needed energy and hope for the future. Although every step-parent has the potential to heal a broken family, this is particularly true for those of us who settle down with someone who has been widowed, as this stepmother's story illustrates:

> Right from the start, the children were very open towards me. They were only six and three, and their daddy took them aside and asked them what they wanted to call me and they both chorused, 'Mummy!', which of course meant a great deal.
>
> I think they were longing to be part of a unit. And not only did the family come together, if you like, but I was able to talk to them about certain things that my husband found too difficult. He really didn't want to discuss their mother, he felt they were too young and it would be too upsetting for them. But in fact they wanted to know some of it. I think it was really about balance. Once they'd got me, their life was more balanced.

This woman was a shining example of how to handle the sensitive issue of a deceased parent. The potential to heal can only be realised if great care is taken over how you personally respond to their bereavement.

Allowing space for the grief of a partner and a stepchild can be problematic. What is left of this person is cherished until it glows. Their reputation takes on an unreal quality. On the one hand, you know that you do not measure up, but on the other hand there is the sense that the comparison is itself weightless: life cannot compare to death.

Although their departed parent will always be hugely significant to your stepchildren, the position of mother or father is technically vacant. A step-parent is thus not a third leg but one of two people who parent. This was explained to me by a stepmother who said:

> Melanie will always be the boys' natural mother but obviously since she died this is not a connection that can give them anything in the way of attention and love. It's actually easier for them to focus on the mother who can give them these things, rather than yearning for this relationship which can never happen.
>
> So although in the beginning there's this tendency to talk about Melanie, after a while it seemed to me that this wasn't helping, like everyone was shoving it down the boys' throats that they'd been deprived of this important thing, instead of moving on. Now instead of calling her Mummy-in-heaven they refer to her as Melanie. And they're settled with what they do have. Everybody says that they're happy kids now.

When a Parent Is Alive But Entirely Absent

It is quite an ordeal for a child to cope with the reality of a biological parent who is out there somewhere but not in contact. Usually it is fathers rather than mothers who lose contact with their natural children, often causing painful feelings of abandonment as a result.

A child in this position still has the impulse to acknowledge this person who is so completely lacking from their lives. The potential for a relationship in the future overlaps with every child's need to feel certain about their biological parents.

A step-parent coming into a situation of this kind does not have to cope with dealing with an ex who is still on the scene, which is in itself a certain freedom. But just because the ex has no reality for the step-parent, this does not mean they lack reality for the stepchild. One stepfather of twelve years said that he felt this keenly with his stepson:

> I was very lucky that Nathan's dad was not around at all. He travels all over the world and has never found the time to see his son. But Nathan never wanted to call me Dad, he's got this nickname for me instead. Having said that, when it comes to other people, he does refer to me as Dad.

When a child has no access to a living biological parent, this can have quite an impact on their psychological make-up. The ability to trust in somebody new is undermined, as Visher and Visher observed: 'If the father abandoned the child, that child may be suspicious of any new father-figure and assume that he too will eventually abandon the family.'[1]

From the step-parent's point of view, the void around their biological counterpart often appears advantageous. But the advantage is less clear-cut than it seems, as a child needs to protect the threads of his or her natural heritage.

When the Ex Is Part of Your Life

Continually coming into contact with your partner's ex often represents a massive struggle. Although technically an outsider, this person has enormous influence over the tenor of your stepfamily life. No matter who has primary care of your stepchildren, you are bound to know precisely what the ex feels about both you and your partner and about your life together as a couple. The ex has direct power over his or her children and their ability to accept a new step-parent. Sadly, it is a power that is often abused.

Once again, a new step-parent is at the mercy of events way beyond their control. The nature of the relationship breakdown determines the magnitude of the task ahead: a broken-hearted ex can foul up what we are trying to achieve, whereas an ex who has moved on can actually facilitate the acceptance of a step-parent.

Fortune can smile on the lucky few; one stepmother I interviewed was a living model of great step-parenthood. Her stepfamily was framed by a joint-custody agreement which stipulated that the children divided their time equally between the houses of their mother and father, spending half the week with each one. This was possible not only because both parents lived near to each other but also because of the nature of their split.

Although Eric was in a mess when Angela asked him for a divorce, he picked himself up again and six months later we started going out. Angela was delighted, because she'd been feeling guilty about ending their marriage. Suddenly everything evened out between her and Eric. The kids got used to having me around for half the week and everything was ticking along nicely.

After a while, Angela asked me to go for a meal, the two of us on our own. She said to me, 'I want you to know that you're the best stepmother I could ever hope for for my children.' It was such a gracious thing to say.

Most of us however have to pick our way through the debris of painful breakdowns which continue to cause hurt to at least one or possibly both parties. Particularly when children are involved, it's impossible to escape unscathed from a relationship breakdown. We may like to believe that our partners have swept away all the unhappy clutter of their former experience, and yet we know that the wounds of the past are easily reopened, especially when the ex crops up.

Although most step-parents try to keep out of the crossfire between ex-spouses, the consequences of their fraught exchanges are plain for all to see. Virtually every conversation leaves one or both parties fuming with anger or mown down with anxiety, depression or frustration. How can we feel neutral about someone who makes our partner so damned miserable?

But there is far more to our resentment than simply being protective of our loved one. Most step-parents feel threatened to a greater or lesser degree by the ex. We are well aware of just how much mental damage they can cause, not only to ourselves but to our partner and the future happiness of our stepfamily.

Here are just some of the reasons that the ex impinges on our well-being:

- Most step-parents tend to feel competitive with an ex who is still on the scene
- Often the approaches of parent and step-parent are in conflict, which is difficult to resolve
- We resent the fact that the ex will always and inevitably be part of our lives and is also a factor in our finances. Whether the ex makes or receives payments or fails to contribute altogether, this involvement or lack of it gives them a power that is often problematic
- The ex is rarely happy about the scale either of the support they receive or the contribution they make. Although technically a third party, it's difficult for a step-parent to keep calm about this ongoing source of conflict. We are uncomfortable because we are powerless
- The ex's opinion not only of our partner but also of ourselves is something beyond our control
- The ex may try to turn our stepchildren against us

It is important to stay calm and follow some ground rules:
- No matter what the ex says about us and our stepfamily, we are not going to respond in kind
- We have to respect a child's need to believe the best about their mother and father

- Letting off steam about the ex should be done behind closed doors, to your partner alone, out of earshot of the others
- The aim here is conceal your true feelings from *all* of the children, both your own if you have them and your stepkids. Don't expect children to keep secrets from each other because they can't

The Double Life of a Stepchild

In the early days of my research, an older stepmother shared a confidence with me that came as something of a revelation. Unusually perhaps, both she and her daughter had become both mothers and stepmothers, comparing notes along the way. From the pool of their shared wisdom, she had drawn the following conclusion:

After a nasty divorce, children are driven by the idea that they should shield their mum from their dad and their dad from their mum so that nobody gets hurt. What they see is that dad gets tense if they talk about mum and vice versa.

To stop everyone from fighting all over again, these kids have chosen not to even mention one 'side' to the other 'side'. When they're not with their dad, they just put that dad life in a box and keep it secret. But this is such an enormous effort for a child to make.

And yet many parents don't even notice. They're quite happy in their not-so-secret dislike of the ex and don't bother to think of the impact this has on the kids. These poor kids compensate by making sure their absent mum or dad is kept well out of the firing range. But this is a real strain.

The best thing that you can do is allow a child of divorce to be happy in both homes. Don't fill him with ideas about his moron dad or stupid mum. Broken hearts and bad blood get in the way, I know. But giving your child permission to be happy in two homes is the greatest gift.

In the unhappy climate that follows on from divorce, a child harbours enormous guilt about needing and enjoying the company of whichever parent happens to be absent at the time. It can feel as if loving their dad is a betrayal of their mum and vice versa. They keep their lives separate to protect the absent parent, as observed by another stepmother:

> We went on holiday to Corsica a couple of years ago and my stepdaughter got ill. Not seriously ill, but she had a temperature and I was worried it might be tonsillitis.
>
> So I called out the doctor and actually it was fine but still she wasn't well so I said, 'Do you want to ring Mummy?' because you always want your mummy when you're sick. And she said yes but she waited until I had left. If there wasn't all this tension, I might've spoken to her mum too, just telling her that Sarah's fine and so on. But as it was, I knew that Sarah was waiting for me to leave the room. It's gut-wrenching, the communication block.

These children are making up their own code of conduct to regulate the post-divorce landscape: neither parent nor stepparent can be entirely trusted as regards the other parent. Convincing your stepchildren that you are quite relaxed about their absent mummy or daddy is settling a critical issue. Although warmth and friendliness about the ex is not an obvious reflex, being broadly inclusive of this person greatly increases your chances of stepfamily success.

A child should not have to feel secretive, embarrassed or ashamed of their absent parent. If you or your partner openly bad-mouth the ex, you are damaging your prospects as a stepfamily. There is a time and a place for venting frustration but it is a high-security operation which demands the 100 per cent guaranteed absence of all kids. Which is preferable: that the adults make the effort or that the stepchildren are forced to lead double lives? The answer is the same, whether or not the ex is out to get you.

When an Ex Has an Axe to Grind

When an ex is still waging war, it becomes a superhuman challenge to suppress the instinct to fight back.

The means and methods of attack are legion. The direct approach is when the ex pitches right into face-to-face confrontation and doesn't hold back. Then there's the indirect approach, which is to deploy the children as middle men in a feud that has nothing to do with them. Regrettably, many an ex involves his or her kids to fight their own personal battles. One stepfather I interviewed took the matter into his own hands when his wife's ex started spreading malicious rumours about him:

> They'd broken up about three years before I came along. But Martin couldn't stand it, my being with Lynn. He was jealous of me, really, really jealous. Next thing I knew, he only told his son that I was a drug dealer. Not only that, but that I sold drugs to *kids*. Johnnie was about nine! What was he meant to think?
>
> That night when Johnnie came back to us, he was strange – you know, awkward, fidgety. Eventually we got it out of him, exactly what Martin had said. I was so angry. I really wanted to go round then and there and sort him out, but I left it. But when I bumped into Martin, it was a while later, I couldn't help it. I was seething. I threatened him, you know, saying that if he ever said anything like that again, it was going to be no holds barred. Well, that was end of the lies . . .

This stepfather managed effectively to tackle the prejudice of the ex head-on. For most of us, such an opportunity is neither available or advisable. We might dream about dismantling the ex's propaganda machine, but when push comes to shove there is little we can do about it. Once again the conscientious step-parent will hold his or her tongue, even when they are the object of an ex's scorn. Although it can be hard swallowing what the ex is serving up, this has to be done if you are to consolidate what you and your partner are trying to achieve.

This was the heartfelt opinion of one woman who felt frustrated as arrangements to see her husband's children for contact weekends would often fall through. The ex had custody of two children aged sixteen and fourteen.

> The main problem is that there's such tension between Frankie and his ex-wife. She has been known to deny access at the last moment and this fouls up all our plans. There's absolutely nothing we can do to stop her pulling the plug but it ruins everything.
>
> Frankie and I, we try to have fun with the children on our weekends with them. So this weekend, for instance, we were meant to go to a musical and we'd fixed up lunch with a family who had kids of a similar age. At the eleventh hour, she called the whole thing off. There's always a pretext – this time it was something about the trains.
>
> So Frankie rang up his kids, you know, just to reassure them and to say, 'Look, I wanted you to come, I'm really, really sorry that you can't come, it's because Mummy and I have had an argument and it's not your fault.' And Daniel, this big fourteen-year-old boy, started crying. It's just heartbreaking. Of course my dealings with my stepchildren are completely overshadowed by the relationship between the parents. I tread on eggshells.

Unfortunately many step-parents become the unwitting focus of the ex's attention. Just as a step-parent feels competitive with the ex, the ex feels competitive with the new partner. Each believes that the other is encroaching on their territory and rivalry runs high.

What You Signify to the Ex

When the ex is proving to be something of a headache, it's worth remembering that despite appearances to the contrary you are not powerless in this dynamic. Your power lies in your partnership.

When an ex is still in turmoil, the reality of your sexual relationship will in one way or another be contributing to their angst. Because we feel to a greater or lesser degree threatened by the ex, it suits our purposes to forget that they in turn are feeling threatened by us.

A step-parent is a strange phenomenon for the ex, as he or she has access to the ex's children when the ex is not around. This fact alone is enough to make an ex agitated and jealous as they are left to ponder the unknown quantity of the person who is now looking after their kids.

Just before my first holiday with my stepdaughters, I met my husband's ex-wife. Understandably enough, she wanted to verify for her own peace of mind that this stranger was going to be up to the job. Beforehand I was very nervous but actually she was equally nervous. For some reason, step-parents often close their eyes to this truth. We prefer to concentrate on what we receive from the ex, almost relishing the drama that they provide.

In fact, the ex is suffering too. When you feel at the end of your tether, it's worth remembering that relations with the ex are not a one-way street. As adults, we should try to cut the ex some slack.

Dove-tailing With the Ex

A child of divorced parents has a primary existence with his or her primary carer and a secondary existence with the absent parent. Whichever category you and your partner fall into, the pair of you have to deal with the consequences of the ex's parenting style. This can raise all sorts of practical problems, which fuel a step-parent's already active resentment of the ex.

The following is a list of some of the most common complaints that step-parents make against their biological counterparts:

The Ex-husband

1. He is unreliable and often lets the children down by being late or failing to show up altogether
2. He is shifty and unpredictable when it comes to making arrangements, and gives insufficient notice about dates etc.
3. Most divorced fathers do not have custody of their biological children and consequently are likely to spoil their children during contact. This can be resented by the counterpart stepfather, who is unable to match this level of indulgence and fears that his own contribution will thus be overshadowed
4. He fails to instil any kind of morality in his offspring, avoiding difficult issues such as discipline
5. He fails to show any real interest in the children's education, and knows nothing about their school life, their friends or hobbies
6. The biggest beef is usually about money: that the ex fails to make proper financial provision for his kids (maintenance for an ex-wife ceases upon her remarriage)
7. A stepfather can feel angry about the comfortable finances

of an ex-husband, especially if he himself is struggling to support his stepfamily

The Ex-wife

1. She is too taken up with her own affairs at the expense of her children
2. Single or remarried, she is often criticised for being bitter about the break-up
3. She is often seen as needlessly extravagant and a drain on the father's wallet
4. She is distrusted for employing the children to ask Dad directly for more money
5. Many stepmothers feel angry about the ex's attitude towards the maintenance that she receives, especially if this is an ongoing source of tension

Dealing with an ex-husband or wife requires enormous care from both you and your partner. The belief that the ex is somehow not pulling their weight is clearly built into most step-parents' coping mechanisms. Stepmothers tend to feel that they have higher standards generally than a stepchild's actual mother. Obviously this stems from a deep-seated feeling of competition and has little basis in reality.

Of all the stepmothers I interviewed, there was only one who did not fault the mothering of her counterpart. As the American psychologist Lillian Messinger observed, the lot of the single mother can be oppressive: 'Her reward is not the same when the family's not all there', and this truth goes some way towards explaining lower domestic standards in the single-parent family. Messinger concludes, 'What right do you have to judge what kind of mother your husband's ex-wife is?'[2]

Remember the split personality of a step-parent discussed in Chapter 8. This principle should be applied not only to our stepchildren but also to their absent parent. Sometimes it's important to stand back and admit to yourself that the ex is probably doing his or her best in the circumstances.

Unless directly involved in their break-up, the new partner has no guilt when it comes to the ex. Although we can feel guilty about the way we deal with our stepchildren, we rarely feel remorse about out attitudes towards our counterpart. In other words, there is no check on the compulsion not only to compete with the ex but also to win.

When you look at your stepchildren and feel proud of them, like it or not a large part of the credit goes to your counterpart. So exercise a little tolerance here; trying to rebuild a life torn apart by divorce is hard. Perhaps you too have been through something similar.

Another peculiar aspect of a step-parent's dealings with the ex is that often a step-parent cares far more violently than his or her own partner about the ex's behaviour. Most divorcees accept a modicum of blame over their marriage breakdown, which translates into an albeit slender capacity to forgive, to cut some slack for their ex-partner. Their new partner however is often quite unable to exercise any forgiveness. One remarried man interviewed told me how his ex-wife's new husband liked to hurl abuse at him down the phone:

> Regular as clockwork, literally on the day the maintenance was due, I'd get this abusive phone call from Samantha's husband. Right off, he'd be shouting, 'Where's the money? Why haven't you paid it in? Why's it late again? Do we really have to put up with this?'
>
> The irony was that the maintenance was never late. It went out of my account automatically and arrived in their bank account on time every time. The guy didn't even bother to check if the money was in. It was like he just wanted to sound off and by God, did he sound off . . .

In most cases, the incoming step-parent has never had a relationship with the ex, yet manages to outstrip his or her partner in
the bitterness stakes. Surely this is a little excessive. We need to
correct the imbalance here and follow our partner's cue. Because
we are one half of a team and because we are loyal, we do not
want to interfere in our partner's delicate relationship with his or
her ex.

This puts a step-parent in a quandary. Frequently there are no
open channels of communication between the ex and a step-
parent, and therefore no means of discussing your stepchildren,
even though this is something you may long to do. A step-parent
can only have a relationship with his or her counterpart if all three
parties have some kind of consensus. If one party is lukewarm, it
simply isn't going to happen.

This is not to say it's impossible. The joint-custody stepmother
quoted on page 109 told me that the mother of her stepchildren
was a real asset when it came to their shared domestic arrangements:

> There was one hilarious time when I took my seven-year-old step-
> daughter, Faithie, swimming. She's always been much more
> self-contained than her brother but that day she sort of rebelled.
> We were in the changing rooms and I was asking her to get
> changed and suddenly she shouted, 'You can't tell me what to do
> because you're *not* my mum!'
>
> I said, 'That's a fair point,' but by total fluke, her mum was in
> the swimming pool at the same time. She literally popped up from
> the next booth and went, 'I know she's not your mother, Faithie,
> but I am! So do what she says, OK?' It was a classic moment,
> unbelievably brilliant. And of course Faithie had to do as she was
> told.

When it comes to making arrangements, women can actually
prefer to talk directly to their counterpart, bypassing the middle

man. These days, my opposite number is happy enough to deal with me. We cut to the chase in a way that can be hard between two divorcees.

The nature of your exchanges with your counterpart is tied in to their personal happiness. If the ex has reached some kind of internal equilibrium smooth relations are more likely. On the other hand, if the ex is still seething about the breakdown of his or her marriage this can be a massive obstacle. Either way, you owe it to your stepchildren to be totally generous about their absent mum or dad.

Putting on the Gloss

Whatever the particulars of your scenario, give your stepchildren the freedom to love their dad when at their mum's or their mum when at their dad's. Children are canny. They pick up on every nuance of your manner. The language that you use in talking about the absent parent, the tone, the inflections and the emotional under-currents will all be noted by your stepchildren. So don't be sloppy.

As discussed at the beginning of this chapter, children from broken homes tend to keep their double lives separate, fearing the consequences of eliding the two. These kids are actively looking for signs that they are right in doing this. The slightest criticism of the ex confirms their prejudice that you cannot be trusted, that Mum is best kept away from Dad and vice versa.

It can take a long time for your stepchildren to relax about the attitude of you and your partner towards their absent parent. But if you both exercise discretion, in time they will. Nobody likes to feel that their own mother or father is disliked. So if you do har-bour a whole lot of negativity towards the ex, whether reasonably founded or not, just make the effort to hide it. Your stepchildren need to feel that nobody's going to get hurt if the subject of their absent parent comes up.

Accept that the ex is part of your extended stepfamily; it's only natural that you should ask a few questions about how they're doing, in a neutral, friendly kind of way.

Being positive about your opposite number can be enormously healing for your stepchildren and thus for your whole stepfamily. It may be a while before you're actually sharing jokes with the ex, but if and when that day ever comes it'll be a great boon for everyone.

11

The Fourth Cornerstone:
Your Stepchildren Need Your Love

When on the receiving end of a whole lot of flak, whether physical danger or emotional turmoil, it's human nature to retreat, pull in the feelers and wait for the stress levels to die down. The discouraged step-parent longs to roll up into a ball like a hedgehog, hoping that the trouble will pass.

Being scorned or treated with hostility makes us believe that our input is not required. In fact the opposite is true. Instead of retreating, we need to push ourselves into being open and giving. Despite appearances to the contrary, a step-parent is somebody of real significance to his or her stepchildren.

In adjusting to the fact that YOU AND YOUR PARTNER ARE A TEAM, your stepchildren are forced to acknowledge that you are a powerful figure in their family. For they understand the basics of an adult partnership and know that you have tremendous influence over their mum or dad. And because virtually all children have reservations about acquiring a step-parent, they fear how you will use that influence. It's your job to calm their considerable fears on this score.

Our stepchildren are quite sure what they think of us. For the reasons detailed in Chapter 9, these youngsters often *need* to harbour negativity towards a step-parent whom they can blame for their own problems. They imagine that their take on us will determine our attitude towards them, and this belief that we will mirror their negativity becomes a great source of anxiety to a child, who knows that a step-parent has peculiar access to their mum or dad. What will you do? Will you slander their good name?

Before a step-parent arrives, interaction with all and sundry is straightforward: if you like someone, it's easy to be nice and hope that they'll like you back. If you want something from someone, you switch on the charm. But what does a stepchild want from a step-parent? This question is often difficult for them to answer. A child's approach is predetermined by a whole host of factors. They are scarcely able to control their attitude towards you; do they want to be liked by you? Or keep you away? But if they keep you away, will you use your influence over your partner to turn Mummy or Daddy against their own child?

The only outcome that a stepchild truly desires is to be allowed to continue his or her relationship with Mum or Dad uninterrupted. This is the conundrum that perplexes many a stepchild: they need something from you, namely that you do not interfere in their time with their parent, but they have great difficulty modifying their attitude to you in order to secure that goal. Because the usual principle of being nice to someone if you want something from them is distorted by their need to be hostile, a stepchild frets that he or she will be deprived of the one thing they really yearn for: their parent.

If stepchildren are adults themselves, their relationships with their natural parents will have settled foundations which can better withstand the arrival of a step-parent. But until a youngster reaches maturity, he or she will continue to nurse secret doubts about what you will do and how and when you will do it. To many kids, a step-parent is a bomb that could go off at any time.

This sense of fear was apparent again and again in interviews with men and women who had grown up with a step-parent. Despite years of stepfamily life, residual doubts often linger, and can even turn into an almost physical alarm. Witness the testimony of one woman:

> I found my stepfather very frightening. He was one of those people who has a very physical presence. I felt that he might thump me at any moment, which was ridiculous because he never, ever came anywhere close to hitting me. But I was very frightened of him all the same.

It all boils down to trust; a natural parent can be trusted but a step-parent is a different matter.

To a greater or lesser degree, we are all aware of our step-children's suspicion. The question is whether we are going to let their mistrust determine our attitude. Are we going to be calm and warm even towards someone who is pushing us away?

Dismantling Paranoia

It takes a long time to acquire confidence as a step-parent, but once you're comfortable with the role, you can tackle the thorny issue of the stepchildren's lack of confidence in you. For stepchildren are vulnerable, more vulnerable than children from unbroken homes.[1] They are more likely to be socially maladjusted and extra support in this regard may well be necessary.

Hopefully their faith in you is already on the increase thanks to the first three cornerstones. In eradicating jealousy by turning to a supportive partner, and in keeping back instead of pitching in, and by keeping rejection at arm's length, you are now behaving with a sure-footed calm. Now for the final hurdle: what do your stepchildren actually need from you?

None of us should give in to a stepchild's disinterest. They can put on whatever front they like, but a stepchild benefits from your involvement. Even when certain that attempts at kindness and affection will be repelled, don't be put off. All youngsters are needy in this regard. Nobody is immune to positive feedback, especially not a child or adolescent still learning about the world.

It's not just step-parents who wrestle with this dynamic. Biological parents also have to deal with turbulent teenagers resentful of authority on the journey to independence. Natural parents find this phase truly trying but they do not switch off the support, praise and love. Here again we might envy the instinct that enables a parent to keep knocking at a closed door. But step-parents are more prone to self-doubt. If they see that the door is closed, they take that as enough of a sign that further contact is not required and beat a hasty retreat.

Being young is a difficult business. It's easy to paint yourself into a tight emotional corner and not so easy to get out. Help, even from a step-parent, is exactly what a troubled kid needs. Small overtures and tiny gestures are noticed and valued by even the most hostile of stepchildren. And when none are forthcoming, progress is impossible, as this account makes clear:

> If my stepmother had said . . . well, it would only have taken a few words, then things might have turned out differently. But she kept quiet. It would only have taken a hug or a phrase like 'It must be awfully hard having me around.' Then I would have just melted.
>
> As it was there was this barrier: both of us had misgivings which festered away. She never offered to help me at all, even

when I was at crisis point. I'd broken up with my husband and my life was a mess. I was longing for her to say, 'Sweetie, if there's anything I can do, just give me a ring,' but she never did. It was like she didn't care.

If you do care for your stepchildren, you have to have the guts to make this explicit in whatever way seems appropriate. For a stepchild isn't going to assume that you love them. Quite the reverse, in fact.

As the adult, it's up to you to dispel their anxieties and communicate the good stuff as soon as, if not before, you feel ready. Override any nerves about whether or not your input will be thrown back in your face. Just seize the initiative; no matter how small and irrelevant the gesture or compliment seems to you, it will probably be of real value to your stepchild.

This truth was brought home to me by an episode involving one of my stepdaughters. This youngster had always kept her distance and I'd assumed that she wanted me to do the same. We'd just returned home from our holidays together and when I got my photos, I sent some on to my stepdaughter along with a nondescript card. When the girls came to stay the following weekend, I asked if the photos had gone down well. In a non-committal kind of way, she said yes. But then almost by accident I learned that the card I'd written was now treated as a prized possession, kept in her 'special box' hidden under her bed. I was amazed and unbelievably touched that this very ordinary message had become a memento to this little girl. It made me reassess my whole approach. Up until then, it had never occurred to me that this child was interested in me in any way. Imagining that she was shut off to anything I had to offer, I had in fact offered her very little. But now I had the confidence to be attentive in ways that I'd previously discounted. Like anyone else, she responded to the attention, even though this was not the message that she was projecting.

In the uncertain environment that is a newly formed step-family, the details really do count. Although stepchildren have their prejudices, this does not stop them from being blind to your good qualities. On one level, they are looking for evidence that can be used to combat negative assumptions. Even a youngster can appreciate that it's better to have a good guy as a step-parent than a bad guy. All you have to do is give them a few shreds of evidence that you are indeed a goodie.

This was summarised for me by a man who had been brought up by his father and stepmother from the age of eight. He came to live with them as he was about to begin a new school, which he was dreading. He remembered being surprised by an act of devotion that occurred soon after his first term had started:

> The whole thing was so foreign to me, this formal, rather uptight new school with this prim uniform. I realised that I was the only boy with short socks and I mentioned this to Nadia, but casually, not making a big deal of it.
>
> And bingo – long socks turned up twenty-four hours later. Nadia had driven right up to London to get them and that was a very heartening gesture to me as a child. The length of my socks wasn't actually a big deal to me, but Nadia considered that I might be worried by it and so she took the trouble to fix it. That was the kind of thing that made you feel that she was there and could be relied on.

And this perhaps is our ultimate goal: we want to be relied upon because that implies not only trust but acceptance too. It's like running for an Academy Award nomination: you're not eligible for the Best Parent Oscar but you are eligible for Best Supporting Role. We should have the confidence to come out of the shadows and into the limelight as someone who is there to provide stability, support and love.

Being True to Yourself

Nobody is suggesting that you whip yourself up into an overbearing frenzy of excessive consideration, like the supercalifragilisticexpialidocious step-parent mentioned in Chapter 7. Every relationship is a law unto itself, a link between two unique characters. We have to gauge the individuals that we are dealing with, just as we have to stay true to ourselves.

At first glance, it may look like there is conflict between the second cornerstone – KNOW YOUR ROLE – and the fourth cornerstone – YOUR STEPCHILDREN NEED YOUR LOVE. But the two are not in opposition. Rather they have a chronological order which must be respected.

A step-parent must first learn to detach, stand back and let the bioparent get on with the business of being a parent. It's only once we have reached the understanding that our stepchildren do not need us remotely like they need their parent that we can get to grips with the nature of the contribution that we can and should make.

Only you can decide how you want to express your interest in and concern for these youngsters. Whether you find it easier to communicate your affection through practical gestures or direct words of praise, by delicate hints or open declarations, all that matters is that you coax yourself into being giving without getting bogged down in the possibility of an adverse reaction.

Practical Exercise

Resolutions are statements of future intention. If we've sunk into bad habits, a reminder of what we hope to achieve is a great way to kick-start a better approach. Create your own personal incentive by asking yourself the following questions:

1. How openly can you be positive towards your stepchildren?
2. How often do you give them encouragement? Or pay them a compliment? Or provide reassurance?
3. Be honest about your stepchild's frailties. Are you aware of particular vulnerabilities? Are there issues that may get overlooked in the business of daily life?
4. Are there any key ways in which you could address their concerns?
5. Framing your objectives is a two-stage process: a) Remind yourself of the positives that you feel, e.g. 'I love little Johnnie because he makes me laugh.' b) Remind yourself of what you want to achieve, e.g. 'Next time I see him, I'm going to tell Johnnie that he's a great kid'
6. These affirmations are for your ears only. They are private, to be repeated and redeveloped as relationships grow

Just telling yourself in total solitude that you love your stepchildren paves the way for being able to communicate this to them when you are ready.

A dash of encouragement can be a revolutionary commodity, opening up all sorts of previously blocked channels. Being the outsider frees you up to be the agent of change. There is no loss of face on your part if a compliment rolls off the tongue, but for stepchildren, pride often gets in the way. So take the initiative. In the long run, everybody will be grateful.

Letting Your Stepchildren Be Their Own People

Loving your stepchildren means loving them as they are, not as you would like them to be. The instinct to shape and mould and protect a child is there for both biological and step-parents.

Without our realising it, much of parenting and step-parenting is about transmitting our own value-systems to the young. Obviously this has its advantages when we pass on some kind of morality, but too much interference is a hazard to be avoided, especially for step-parents.

It's hard for a step-parent to keep this grooming impulse in check. We begin life with our stepchildren as the outsider and we over-compensate, pedalling furiously to catch up. Coming to terms with the fact that we will never catch up is territory covered by the second cornerstone: KNOW YOUR ROLE. But we want them to do better at music or football, learn French or go travelling, stop smoking marijuana or cut their hair. In fact we are full of wants, and these can be immensely damaging. It is the remit of the fourth cornerstone to draw a line under such excessive interference.

It is neither appropriate nor constructive for a step-parent to become obsessed with securing specific goals for their stepchildren. When you leave the realm of general care and find yourself thinking, 'If only Johnnie was more . . .' or 'I wish Madeleine could . . .' it is time to pull yourself up short and examine what exactly you are doing.

In foisting your aspirations on to a stepchild, you are overstepping the mark in ways that he or she will be painfully aware of even if you are not. This was another lesson that I learned the hard way. One of my stepdaughters is into computer games, horror movies and heavy metal, all of which leave me cold. I felt threatened by her and she in turn felt threatened by me. Without realising what I was doing, I began to lay down rules about how she could spend her time. I banned PlayStation, restricted her use of other computer games and disapproved of her vampire books. I was trying to make her more like me.

This was of course doomed to fail. She is strong-willed and resented my interference like hell. Eventually I realised that I was being too controlling, and that I had to accept her particular tastes.

What did it matter if she was into Grand Theft Auto and Vlad the Impaler?

Most relationships are based on what people have in common – a sense of humour, the same take on life. Some relationships are founded on interaction at work or with people in shops, in the street, service providers. And then there is the blood-family bond. The trouble with the step dynamic is that it isn't included in any of the above groups. It is a relationship that is not based on shared values, is neither a blood tie nor a love affair, but exists right at the heart of your life.

Step-parents are confused by the alien nature of the step dynamic and find themselves believing that they can only get on with their stepchildren if they hammer out something in common. We all know that it's easier to get along with someone when our interests overlap, but what the step dynamic requires is a friendship that is based on proximity, on steady affection rather than shared values. Although natural mothers and fathers meddle in their children's habits, this is underwritten not only by their prerogative as parents but also by their acceptance of their offspring come what may, axe-murderers or angels.

Instead of manufacturing an artificial bond by madly squeezing out some shared territory, we should relax and learn to embrace our stepchildren as they truly are, warts and all. Working with what you've got is infinitely easier than endlessly struggling with a hopeless project. For your stepchildren are not a project, they are people in their own right.

A few step-parents get to know their stepchildren before they ever meet their future partner. Such circumstances make it easier to appreciate individual natures, free from the distorting lens of the step dynamic. One stepfather relayed just how impressed he'd been by two children whose mother was elsewhere:

I met the kids before I knew Cecile; it was at their grandparents' house in Wales. And I was struck by them. I remember thinking that they were some of the nicest children I'd ever come across. I'd heard about Cecile from various people, and after I met these kids I thought to myself, I'd love to meet their mum. Of course I never did anything about it. But a year later, by chance we were all back at the grandparents' house and there was Cecile with her kids . . . and there I was . . . and, well, now here we are.

In many ways, this is the ideal order of events. A first encounter occurs without knowing that at some distant point this individual will become your stepchild. A mutual appraisal goes on, as is always the case when meeting a stranger, but this process is the same with this person as with any other. It is not complicated by the looming presence of a third party, the pivotal figure of parent and partner, unwittingly turning on the pressure to be liked and to succeed as a step-parent.

If you ask me, the future Maria von Trapp had it easy in *The Sound of Music*, endearing herself to the captain's brood as a governess rather than as his lover. The gaggle of mini-Trapps fell in love with Maria long before Papa succumbed to her charms. If only the rest of us were blessed with such a beginning!

Working Out What You Have to Offer

In the end every step-parent reaches his or her own understanding of what he or she has to offer. This is a personal business, as the step-parent develops a better sense of the particular needs of each stepchild. There are however a few constants which are woven into the fabric of any strong relationship:

- Trust
- Stability
- Security

This trio of positives cannot be forced into existence. They grow as a reward for the considerate individual who takes pride in behaving well. We earn the trust of our stepchildren slowly, by demonstrating that we will not obstruct their time and space with their parent. And as this pattern of standing back is repeated again and again, their trust in us is reinforced. Rather than being unpredictable, we are a recognised, known quantity and a source of stability. When this awareness dawns, it makes a visible impression on a stepchild, who finally realises that having us around is a good thing and that in our own way we contribute to their security.

Step relationships can take on the qualities of other established relationships, as we subconsciously model this interaction on patterns that are familiar to us, some of which are detailed below.

Step-parent as Co-parent

If you are comfortable with the responsibilities involved in parenting, you may slide into mothering or fathering a stepchild, treating them as you would treat your own kids. But as the second cornerstone, KNOW YOUR ROLE, made explicit, we are most definitely not on a par with bioparents and should not indulge any fantasies about being 'like a mother' or 'like a father' unless our stepchildren are happy for us to share in the parenting glory. You have to exercise discretion and not steamroll into the sacred preserve of natural parenthood. On the surface you may fulfil all the criteria, but don't get confused. Being a co-parent is something quite separate.

Step-parent as Uncle/Aunt

This is an accurate model respecting the divide between older and younger generations. It also places a step-parent within the

extended-family nexus but outside the tight-knit unit of the biological family. By analogy, the step-parent is at once included and
excluded, and this is a true of reflection of step-parenthood. From
a child's point of view, an aunt or uncle is an extension of their
parent in much the same way that the new partner is also an
extension of their parent. Your right to be there is undeniable and
yet you are at one remove, a secondary source of support and
love. But this is not to demean what can be a tremendously powerful bond. Avuncular input, affection and interest is a great asset
to anyone, providing direction and hope in times of uncertainty. It
is a useful benchmark for a step-parent.

Step-parent as Friend/Sibling

When there is a relatively small age gap between step-parent and
stepchild, the closeness in age fosters a sense of somehow being
allies, either as siblings or as pals.

In numerous interviews, both stepchildren and step-parents
described their relationships in this way. The stepdaughter with
the jealous stepmother told me that she none the less felt like this
woman was her big sister. One stepfather liked to josh and jape
with his stepson, nineteen years his junior and an only child. This
man said, 'Nick never had anyone to play with as a kid and when
I came on the scene I felt that he needed a bit of ribbing, gentle
teasing, and that was how it all began.' Obviously both stepfather
and stepson enjoyed this banter, having exploited the unique
opportunity presented by the step dynamic.

All the above relationships imply active involvement, and this is
the key to step-parenting. Your stepchildren do not want you to
loiter for ever in the margins of their lives, holding back and
revealing nothing. Someone who expresses no interest in his or
her stepchildren will always be resented as a complication with no
redeeming features. It's up to you to consider what you can offer

that will be of help to your stepchildren. One stepmother told me:

> The specific thing I could help my stepdaughters with was music. They played the violin and so did I, so we'd practise together, and as we screeched away, that sort of opened up this little world where we'd play a few bars then chat and start again, screeching and chatting.
>
> They'd tell me stuff that they felt they couldn't tell their mum as she would worry too much, or perhaps ask me about stuff that I might know about but their mother didn't know about. The mother and I, well we're very different characters. If the girls wanted my advice, it was always going to have contrast-value.

Practical Exercise

Seeing your stepchildren away from your partner can reveal them to be startlingly different people from those you thought you knew.

1. Try to isolate a hobby, skill, treat or activity that can become the special thing that you do with your stepchild, independent of your partner. Discuss this with your partner: are you in agreement here?
2. Make a note in your Step-parenting Record to find time for this activity. Regardless of what you do together, even something as ordinary as homework, it's the shared endeavour that's important

Getting in the Habit

Loving your stepchildren doesn't come easily when they are antagonistic towards you. But a relaxed and quietly upbeat manner towards those who treat you as the enemy is a strategy that has real potential to make a difference. Put a photograph of a sulky stepson on your desk and see how flattered he is when he notices it's there. Ask your stepdaughter whether you should wear the orange scarf or the polka-dot one. Show them you want them on board.

Discreet support now and then reminds these youngsters that you may not quite be what they think you are. From small beginnings, great things grow. Watch as the effects curl and spread through your stepfamily, dissolving hardened emotions along the way. As anyone in human resources will tell you, being positive is one skill that we cannot afford to do without. Everybody needs encouragement.

12

Reworking the Myth

Not before time, we are finally waking up to the truth that a step-parent can be a positive force in the life of his or her stepchild. As Tolstoy observed, 'All families are happy in the same way'[1] and this is no less true of the stepfamily. A step-parent can heal a fractured family.

And yet the bias against the non-traditional family lingers on. Stepfamilies are themselves often riddled with confusion, with a slippery longing to conform. Witness the following account of one stepfather's nightmare in the build-up to his stepdaughter's marriage.

When Alice's real father said that he was flying over from America for the wedding, everything that we'd planned suddenly collapsed. Up until then, I hadn't troubled too much. I'd been a father to Alice all along. She'd stopped seeing her dad long ago. Their relationship disintegrated really because he was in the States. He's remarried now with young kids and is absorbed with his new life.

That's what sent me round the bend. Richard has his family and quite frankly, I felt he was interfering in *my* family. But what could I do? Everyone seemed to feel, especially my wife, that the spotlight would be on me instead of Alice if I walked her up the aisle when Richard was right there at the front of the congregation. Poor Alice said she would prefer it to be me. But I didn't want to complicate things for her on her big day.

The wedding became an elaborate pretence as far as this stepfather was concerned. He had to listen to his wife's first husband giving the speech, despite the fact that he had played no part in his daughter's life for over twenty-five years. The stepfather felt that it was hypocrisy from beginning to end.

Many children may in fact be receiving more love and attention from a step-parent than from an absent biological parent. This contention is supported by the finding that stepmothers show more interest in their stepchildren's schooling than a natural mother who has married again shows in the schooling of her own biological children.[2] And yet the bias against stepmothers persists. A primary-school teacher, also a stepmother, told me how infuriated she was by this brain-washing:

When you think how many children are either going through divorce or second marriages and have half-siblings or step-siblings, it is mind-blowing that none of this is ever talked about at school. We have to teach all sorts of things under the umbrella of personal and social education, about the environment and so on. But we don't talk to children about the breakdown of relationships.

There should be a programme for us to talk about different family structures. If this was built into the curriculum, we could help children get to grips with some of their problems, like it's OK to love Mummy and Daddy even though they don't live together any more, and it's OK to love your stepmother and it's fine to love your stepbrother as much as your natural sister. You know, they must have all sorts of hang-ups because no one ever talks to them about these things. I think it's a real shame.

Politicians across the board insist on the importance of the family but lack the imagination to include restructured families. They stick to what they know, instinctively defending the tidy unit of a first marriage. Consequently education is 'not yet structured to deal with stepfamilies', as one psychologist observed, adding that 'the stepparent often feels tentative about participating in the school. A lack of inclusion from the school reinforces this tendency and increased withdrawal may follow.'[3] At a time when children are most open to embracing all kinds of new concepts, they are indoctrinated with a single domestic construct. It is a classic lost opportunity. As the stepmother above remarked, this attitude makes it much harder for youngsters. Why should kids be made to feel anxious about loving their step-parents?

Arguably, divorce is more socially acceptable than the stepfamily. The lone parent is seen as normal whereas the step-parent is kept locked up in negative folklore which our culture does nothing to contradict. From *Cinderella* to *Lolita*, a poor stepchild suffers at the hands of a wicked stepmother or abusive stepfather. The stepmother receives the greatest drubbing. However if we analyse the origins of the tradition, it becomes plain that the evil step-parent is nothing more than a literary device.

The fairy tale of *Hansel and Gretel* is an interesting example of such a literary device. In the story a woodcutter, his wife and two children fall upon hard times. There are four mouths to feed and no food. Rather than endure starvation, the parents decide to rid themselves of their children by taking them deep into the forest and leaving them there to fend for themselves. Hansel overhears their plan and comes up with his own plan, and the rest is familiar stuff.

What's less familiar is the fact that in the original it is Hansel's own mother who initiates the debate about ditching the kids. In later versions, Hansel's father is influenced by his second wife, because over time parents recoiled from the idea that a mother could abandon her own children. Such unimaginable betrayal made the story too shocking. Much easier to house all these alien and wicked emotions in a third party, the marginalised figure of the stepmother.

The Brothers Grimm knew human nature well enough to know that a mother is quite capable of turning on her own offspring. But this degree of honesty did not appeal to their readership, mostly young mothers keen to keep it sweet and saintly for their darlings. They exonerated themselves by deciding that a stepmother had to be responsible for such cruel treatment. And because this version was infinitely more palatable to the majority, it gradually replaced the original.

The popular rewriting of *Hansel and Gretel* reflects a wide-spread tendency to shelve the less-than-lovely aspects of our character. Biological parents want to be nothing but goodness through to the core. And so a minority gets dumped on so that the majority can protect their reputation. This is the origin of the wicked-stepmother myth. It is always easier to blame an outsider than ourselves.

This device only worked as long as stepmothers were a small, insignificant minority. Now that we are everywhere, the device ceases to be believable. We can't all be bad, because that would point the finger at the rest of society, so keen to preserve its self-image as whiter than white.

Are Your Stepchildren Your Children?

Not only is the whole language of step-parenting weighed down with negative connotations, but it has also created fixed boundaries about who belongs to whom and why.

In Britain, there is a peculiar insistence that step-parents keep their hands off other people's natural children. Even when a step-parent fills the void left by the death of a biological parent, providing as much support as a mother or father, people are weirdly keen to put the emphasis on the literal truth: that this person is only a step-parent, not a 'real' parent.

All the step-parents that I interviewed who had lived for many years with their stepchildren were in agreement here: as far as they were concerned, their stepchildren *were* their children. In blended stepfamilies, with a second batch of biological children, the conclusion was no different. The quality and character of the blood tie is something special but it does not take precedence over the tie that exists between a step-parent and stepchild. One stepfather explained this to me succinctly:

I have three kids – two stepdaughters and one son of my own – and I love them all the same but in different ways. What I feel for my son is different, but it isn't stronger. If I had to put it into words, it's like an extra layer of deep-down worry that I have for him but don't have for the girls. But that's all it is, a funny deep-seated anxiety. They're all equal, and when the time comes this is made quite clear in the terms of my will.

Clearly a step-parent can feel just as bonded to a stepchild as to a biological child. Similarly, children can be equally or more attached to a step-parent, as the following account of a 1950s childhood demonstrates:

When we were little, my stepfather spent time with us in a way that my mother never did. He found us special things, little daft treasures which he would give to us. Sometimes he went away and I would cry and cry. Home was so much less fun when he was away. My mother just wasn't interested in us like he was. And then she would be nasty to him and I couldn't bear that.

They didn't get along too well, and when she wanted to be spiteful my mother would tell him that we were nothing to do with him. As far as she was concerned we belonged only to her, like we were her property. Seeing how upset he was, you know, because he had no children of his own, it made me want to weep.

Children of course are not the property of their biological parents. They are individuals who need terrific amounts of care, and they are tied to whoever provides that care. We need a value system that reflects this diversity. In order to be taken seriously, custodial step-parents gloss over their real identity to keep it simple. They put in all the work of a father or a mother and often want to claim the title too. If they declared their true colours, they would be marginalised by a society that places no value on step-parenting.

As a non-custodial stepmother, I feel this keenly. Everyone knows how to categorise me as a mother of three, but as a stepmother of two I am much more difficult to process. If I tell someone that I'm a stepmother, this triggers the assumption that these girls belong to someone else, tidying them away from me.

This is the reason that we never use the 'half' prefix to differentiate between my husband's five children. We have three kids together, who don't want to be kept separate from these girls whom they adore. In fact, they want the exact opposite, to all be living together all the time, hugger-mugger.

The tide of prejudice is only going to turn if step-parents stand up for themselves as people who have an important contribution to make. Instead of resigning from a debate that is skewed against us, we need to kick-start a new era which sees us wearing the step-parenting badge with pride.

Increasing Recognition

There is a powerful contrast between attitudes towards step-parents in Britain and attitudes in North America. In the States,

the opinion that step-parents deserve recognition is acknowledged at every level. The weighty network provided by the
Stepfamily Association of America unites a disparate group,
giving advice and creating forums for discussion. There is mer-
chandising aimed specifically at the step market, from greetings
cards to the elaborate medals that step-parents can present to their
stepchild (and vice versa) to 'celebrate' their special relationship.
The government has also responded by designating a specific
'Step-parents' Day' in the calendar, to complement Mothers' Day
and Fathers' Day.

This may sound a little schmaltzy for the more restrained
British taste. But the principle holds good: a step-parent is an
important person to his or her stepchildren. In fact what is usually
considered a drawback, namely the lack of a biological tie, often
turns out to be a bonus. The intensity of the tie between a natural
parent and child has its own complications, as one stepmother
succinctly explained to me: 'One of the pluses, but it seems like a
minus, is that you approach stepchildren very much as people in
their own right. You don't approach them with that complex
umbilical thing. So you're more objective . . .' Step-parents offer a
particular brand of support, one with fewer strings attached. This
is a distinction which I feel myself in relation to my stepchildren
and my biological children. There's always an agenda with the
fruit of your womb; a hefty tangle of values and aspirations and
fears that can be something of a blight. It is an intense bond but an
oppressive one too.

My stepdaughters enjoy a freedom with me that my own offspring do not. This is the heart of the matter: you see your
stepchildren as people, whereas natural children are eternally
trapped in the perspective of a parent. Sometimes I wonder
whether my children wouldn't actually prefer to have me as their
stepmother.

An Asset That Endures

Because a step-parent must work hard to establish a bond with a stepchild, the end result is surprisingly durable. Against some-times overwhelming odds, a real bond has been created between two people who may have started out by loathing one another but have come to place their trust in each other.

A strong tie between step-parent and stepchild defies the age gap. The ways in which we appreciate our stepchildren are not dissimilar from friendship. Stepchildren are an asset, the hidden extra that gives your life a special twist.

The enduring nature of a positive step dynamic can withstand much trauma, outlasting relationship breakdown. In situations where a step-parent is no longer with their stepchild's natural parent, the involvement often remains just as strong.

> We were married for twenty years, but after the break-up I felt very much that I shouldn't muscle in on my husband's children. The children that we'd had together came to live with me and that's why I felt like I had to step back from my stepchildren, to give my husband his space now that we were separated.
>
> But what's been amazing is the way that things with my stepchildren have sprouted up again, like spring after the winter. My strategic absence didn't affect anything. We'd always got along; whenever my stepchildren came to stay, we had a laugh. Now I know we'll always be friends.

The step dynamic is demanding but if you give it the attention, commitment and focus that it needs, you'll be creating a relation-ship that is its own reward. For what appears to be the weakness of the step dynamic is in fact its hidden strength. The only way that we can compensate for beginning with less than zero is to concentrate.

And because all this takes both determination and skill, a

positive step dynamic enhances self-esteem. Research has shown that a stepmother's confidence can actually exceed the confidence of a natural mother,[4] and this has to be because we know we've succeeding in growing something strong on thorny ground. Enjoying your stepchildren is a feather in your cap. It says a great deal of good about everyone in your stepfamily. Above all, you can take pride in what ties you together.

Appendix: Step-parents and the Law

Although the stepfamily is common enough today, legal systems have been slow to recognise this growing phenomenon. The law is reluctant to contemplate overlapping domestic arrangements and all the complications that these entail. The traditional view emphasises the legal responsibility of only two people in the lives of children: their biological parents.

There are few positive presumptions when it comes to stepparents. The classic example is of a step-parent who takes a sickly stepchild to hospital but is not eligible to sign the medical consent forms. Or the custodial stepfamily where the bioparent dies: unless legal steps have already been taken, a step-parent, no matter how devoted, has no claim to the stepchild who has been raised in his or her care. Unprotected in this way, a step-parent could find that the child is removed by the state and placed with the nearest blood relative.

The lack of legal recognition also has inheritance implications, as demonstrated by *In re* Burge's Estate 47 n.W.2d 428 (Minn 1951). The facts of the case stated that Mr Burge had brought up his stepdaughters from the ages of seven and eight respectively, supported them, put them both through school and continued to look after them after their mother had died. He had made verbal statements that he intended to disinherit his blood relatives and to leave all of his property to the girls. Yet when he died without leaving a will, the Supreme Court of Minnesota prohibited his stepdaughters from inheriting anything.

Fortunately, some progress has been made since then (although not in the sphere of inheritance law, which still stipulates that a stepchild must be specifically named in a will in order to inherit). Today there are a number of ways in which a step-parent can legally register his or her commitment to a stepchild. However, these remedies tend to be available only to those step-parents whose partners have custody of the child concerned, thus keeping a large slice of the step-parenting community out in the cold.

In Britain, a custodial step-parent can rely on the concept of 'parental responsibility'. Following the breakdown of a relationship, the court is empowered to make a residence order determining where the child of that relationship shall live. When a residence order is made in favour of a particular bioparent, who then begins cohabiting with a new partner, the new partner can apply to the court for parental responsibility. If a step-parent is granted parental responsibility, he or she then has the legal right to be involved in all decisions relating to the child's welfare and is on an equal footing with anyone else who has parental responsibility.

Recent legislation provides something of a breakthrough for the non-custodial British step-parent. The relevant section of the Adoption and Children Act 2002, due to come into force in September 2005, introduces the 'special guardianship order'. According to Section 115 of the act, if all those who have parental responsibility for a child are in agreement with such an order being made, a step-parent who does not live with his or her stepchild can be made a special guardian. However as this legislation is as yet untested, it is impossible to predict the circumstances in which the court would be prepared to make such an order.

In ascertaining who are the important adults in a child's life, the British courts apply a theoretical test known as 'child of the family' derived from Section 52 of the Matrimonial Causes Act 1973. This is used to determine issues such as maintenance, future contact between step-parent and stepchild in the case of step-family breakdown, as well as inheritance.

The attitude of the Australian courts is in harmony with the British approach. The Family Law Act 1995 empowers the Family Law Court to make a parenting order on a step-parent's behalf. If such an order is granted, the step-parent becomes the joint legal guardian with the child's other legal guardian and/or parent. The procedure insists that if another parent was named on the birth certificate, then that person is advised about the application for a parenting order, in much the same way as all those with parental responsibility must be informed of a step-parent's application for parental responsibility in the United Kingdom.

In the USA however the situation is surprisingly different. In America, the concept of parental responsibility does not exist. Traditionally, the only third-party parental rights recognised by the United States judicial system are those of the adoptive parent, so a step-parent can only be legally acknowledged if they have succeeded in adopting their stepchild. But step-parent adoption is only appropriate in strictly defined circumstances, when a child has a non-existent or negligible relationship with his or her absent bioparent. Thus many step-parents may wish to be legally acknowledged as an important person in the life of a stepchild but will not be eligible to adopt.

In an attempt to create some kind of middle ground, the American courts began to evolve the concept of the 'psychological parent', defined as someone who is not a bioparent but who nevertheless fulfils a parenting role for the child on a day-to-day basis. Clearly this label applies equally well to any third party, from hands-on carers to grandparents and step-parents.

Applying this concept has brought about some positive results for step-parents in certain states, notably in the arena of post-relationship-breakdown contact and custody orders. Relying on the 'psychological parent' model, a step-parent can apply for custody of a stepchild on the same footing as a natural parent. There is no bias in favour of the bioparent; it is simply a matter of deciding which of the applicants is able to provide a superior level of care.

The concept of the 'psychological parent' was an attempt to level the playing field between natural parents and others who can also provide a high level of care for a given child. But this emerging doctrine received a setback in the case of Troxel v. Granville, 530 US 57, 120 S Ct. 2054,147 L.Ed 29 (2000) in which the United States Supreme Court specifically recognised as a fundamental liberty the 'interest of parents in the care, custody and control of their children'. This case has had a devastating effect on the nascent rights of the 'psychological parent'. As the Appeal Court of Oregon stated, 'We understand the law [of Troxel v. Granville] to create a presumption in favor of a natural parent's custody, which may be rebutted by a showing that the natural parent will not provide adequate love and care for the child, or that moving the child to the natural parent's custody will cause undue physical or psychological harm.' Clearly this creates a substantial burden of proof for any would-be custodial step-parent.

Arguably the American stepchild suffers as a result, to quote Dr Margorie Engel, President of the Stepfamily Association of America 2003: 'the existing protection is not adequate for the stepchild who is dependent upon the care along with the emotional and financial support of the step-parent'.

Across the border in Canada, step-parents' legal rights received a boost from the seminal case of Chartier v. Chartier (1999), 1 S.C.R 242. This was a landmark decision by the Supreme Court which held that a step-parent cannot unilaterally terminate a parental relationship with a stepchild. The facts concerned the obligation of a stepfather to continue paying child support after his relationship with the biological mother of his stepdaughter had broken down. In determining that Mr Chartier was bound to continue supporting his stepdaughter, the Supreme Court established a new test for defining who is a parent to any given child, set out as follows:

> The relevant factors in defining a parental relationship include whether a child participates in the extended family in the same way as would a biological child; whether the person provides financially for the child (depending on ability to pay); whether the person disciplines the child as a parent; whether the person represents to the child, the family and the world, that he or she is responsible as a parent to the child; the nature or existence of the child's relationship with the absent biological parent.

This judgement echoes the British test of 'child of the family'. Using the criteria set out in Chartier v. Chartier, any Canadian court is able to reach a conclusion as to who is providing parental care for a child. The broad scope of these criteria is judicial recognition that a child can have more than two fathers or mothers. This judgement is of vital significance as a common-law precedent.

References

Chapter 1: Introduction
1. Pasley, K., and Ihinger-Tallman, M., *Stepparenting: Issues in Theory, Research and Practice*, Connecticut, Praeger, 1994, Chapter 2

Chapter 2: Self-Assessment Questionnaire
1. Dewar, Sir Thomas in *The Mind Gym: Wake Your Mind Up*, London, Time Warner Books, 2005, p. 6

Chapter 3: The Confidence Trick
1. Visher, E., and Visher, J., *Stepfamilies: Myths and Realities*, New York, Citadel Press, 1993, Chapter 12
2. Ibid, Chapter 5
3. Thompson, L., and Walker, A. J. 'Women and Men in Marriage, Work and Parenthood', *Journal of Marriage and the Family*, vol 51, 1989, pp. 845–871

Chapter 4: The First Cornerstone
1. Ephron, D., *Funny Sauce*, New York, Viking Penguin, 1986, pp. 158–159
2. Visher and Visher, *Stepfamilies*, Chapter 12
3. Ephron, D., op cit., p. 161
4. Visher and Visher, *Stepfamilies*, Chapter 5
5. Ibid
6. Lewis, J., *et al.*, *No Single Thread: Psychological Health in Family Systems*, New York, Bruner/Mazel, 1976, p. 210

Chapter 5: Teamwork in Practice
1. Visher and Visher, *Stepfamilies*, Chapter 8
2. Ibid, Chapter 12
3. Ibid
4. Bray, J., in Pasley and Ihinger-Tallman, *Stepparenting*

Chapter 6: Stepfamilies Across the Spectrum

1. Visher and Visher, *Stepfamilies*, Chapter 6
2. Ferri, E., *Stepchildren: A National Study*, London, Routledge, 1984, Chapter 1
3. Ibid
4. Visher and Visher, op. cit., Chapter 6
5. Duberman, L., *The Reconstituted Family: A Study of Remarried Couples and Their Children*, Chicago, Nelson-Hall, 1975, Chapter 8
6. Visher and Visher, op. cit., Chapter 6
7. Ferri, E., op. cit., Chapter 11
8. Visher and Visher, op. cit., Chapter 11
9. Ferri, E., op. cit., Chapter 7
10. Ibid
11. Bohannan, P., 'Stepping In', *Psychology Today*, January 1978
12. Ferri, E., op. cit., Chapter 1
13. Bowerman, C., and Irish, D., 'Some Relationships of Stepchildren to Their Parents', *Marriage and Family Living*, May 1962
14. Ferri, E., op. cit., Chapter 1
15. Visher & Visher, op. cit., Chapter 6
16. Ibid, Chapter 5
17. Nadler, Janice Horowitz, Ph.D. thesis on the psychological stress of the stepmother, 1976
18. Ferri, E., op. cit., Chapter 6
19. Furstenburg, F., *Renegotiating Parenthood After Divorce and Remarriage*, 1981
20. Pasley and Ihinger-Tallman, *Stepparenting*, Chapter 1
21. Duberman, L., op. cit., Chapter 5
22. Watson, P., *Ancient Stepmothers: Myth, Misogyny and Reality*, Brill Academic, 1994, Chapter 1
23. Visher and Visher, op. cit., Chapter 4
24. Ephron, D., *Funny Sauce*, pp. 169–170
25. Pasley and Ihinger-Tallman, op. cit., Chapter 4
26. Duberman, L., op. cit., Chapter 8
27. Visher and Visher, op. cit., Chapter 12
28. The Office of National Statistics, 1998–9: In 5 per cent of stepfamilies a biological father has custody of children from a previous relationship. This corresponds to the findings of Furstenburg and Nord in *Journal of Marriage and the Family*, vol. 47, 1985 which puts the percentage of custodial fathers in the USA between 5 and 10 per cent
29. Visher and Visher, op. cit., Chapter 6
30. Duberman, L., op. cit., Chapter 8

31. Visher and Visher, op. cit., Chapter 1
32. Ibid
33. Ibid, Chapter 12
34. Ibid, Chapter 9
35. Duberman, L., op. cit., Chapter 8
36. Visher and Visher, op. cit., Chapter 6
37. Santrock, J., Warshak R., and Elliott, G., 'Social Development and Parent–Child Interaction in Father Custody and Stepmother Families', in Lamb, M. (ed.) *Nontraditional Families*, 1982
38. Visher and Visher, op. cit., Chapter 11
39. Ferri, E., op. cit., Chapter 1
40. Visher and Visher, op. cit., Chapter 11
41. Ferri, E., op. cit., Chapter 1
42. Visher and Visher, op. cit., Chapter 11
43. Ferri, E., op. cit., Chapter 1
44. Visher and Visher, op. cit., Chapter 11
45. Duberman, L., op. cit., Chapter 8
46. Visher and Visher, op. cit., Chapter 8
47. Duberman, L., op. cit., Chapter 8
48. Ganong, L., and Coleman, M., 'Stepchildren's Perception of Their Parents', *Journal of Genetic Psychology*, vol. 148, 1987
49. Visher and Visher, op. cit., Chapter 2

Chapter 7: The Second Cornerstone

1. Fast, I., and Cain, A., 'The Stepparent Role', *American Journal of Orthopsychiatry*, vol. 36, April 1966, pp. 485–491
2. Draughon, M., 'Stepmother's Model of Identification in Relation to Mourning in the Child', *Psychological Reports*, vol. 36, 1975, pp. 183–189
3. Ephron, D., *Funny Sauce*, p. 172
4. Ibid, pp. 165–167
5. In the UK, the Adoption and Children Act 2002 enables a cohabiting couple who are not married to adopt, and this includes same-sex couples
6. Crosbie-Burnett, M., 'Application of Family Stress Theory to Remarriage', *Family Relations*, vol. 38, 1989, pp. 323–331
7. Pasley and Ihinger-Tallman, *Stepparenting*, Chapter 3
8. Visher and Visher, *Stepfamilies*, Chapter 11

Chapter 8: Realistic Expectations

1. Ferri, E., *Stepchildren*, Chapter 1

Chapter 9: The Third Cornerstone

1. Visher and Visher, *Stepfamilies*, Chapter 13

Chapter 10: The Ex Factor

1. Visher and Visher, *Stepfamilies*, Chapter 6
2. Messinger, L., *Remarriage: A Family Affair*, Kluwer Academic/ Plenum Publishers, 1984

Chapter 11: The Fourth Cornerstone

1. Ferri, E., *Stepchildren*, Chapter 7

Chapter 12: Reworking the Myth

1. Tolstoy, L., *War and Peace*, London, Penguin Books Ltd, 1997, Chapter 1
2. Ferri, E., *Stepchildren*, Chapter 6
3. Brown, D., 'The Stepfamily: A Growing Challenge for Social Work', (SWT Monograph, Norwich, University of East Anglia, 1982)
4. Pasley and Ihinger-Tallman, *Stepparenting*, Chapter 1

Resources

Parentline Plus
Tel: 0207 284 5500 (office hours)
0808 800 2222 (24-hour helpline)
www.parentlineplus.org.uk
email: parentsupport@parentlineplus.org.uk
A British-registered charity that provides support and advice covering all areas of family life.

Relate
Herbert Gray College
Little Church Street
Rugby
CV21 3AP
Tel: 0845 456 1310
0795 188 6662 (emergency helpline)
www.relate.org.uk

Long-established British charity aimed at helping couples through difficult times, offering counselling and courses on marriage.

Stepfamily Association of America
650 J. Street, Suite 205
Lincoln,
NE 68508
Tel: 1 402 477 7837
1 800 735 0329 (toll-free only if calling from within USA)
www.stepfam.org
also see: www.steptogether.org
This established organisation runs a network of meetings in chapters

across the country. Also available to members: access to trained thera-pists and the association's range of media information. Annual membership is about $35 but those outside the USA must send an inter-national money order for their membership to be processed.

Stepfamily Foundation, Inc.
333 West End Ave
New York
NY 10023
Tel: 1 212 877 3244
www.stepfamily.org
email: stepfamily@aol.com
Driven by the dynamic personality of Jeannette Lofas, much information is on offer to help build a successful stepfamily relationship.

The Canadian Stepfamily Foundation
www.angelfire.com/on3/onstep
This website evolved out of the Ontario Stepfamily Association. After some wrangling over nomenclature, this active site goes from strength to strength with much interesting material to be found.

Stepfamily Association of South Australia
PO Box 1162
Gawler
South Australia 5118
Tel: (09) 8522 7007
www.stepfamily.asn.au
email: sasa@stepfamily.asn.au
Comprehensive site with many forums, information and links.

www.geocities.com
A site specifically designed for stepfathers, run by a stepfather in. Australia.

For further information on step-parenting visit:
www.stepparenting.co.uk